Game Programming with Code Angel

Learn how to code in Python on Raspberry Pi or PC

Mark Cunningham

Apress®

Game Programming with Code Angel: Learn how to code in Python on Raspberry Pi or PC

Mark Cunningham
Edinburgh, Scotland

ISBN-13 (pbk): 978-1-4842-5304-5   ISBN-13 (electronic): 978-1-4842-5305-2
https://doi.org/10.1007/978-1-4842-5305-2

Managing Director, Apress Media LLC: Welmoed Spahr
Acquisitions Editor: Aaron Black
Development Editor: James Markham
Coordinating Editor: Jessica Vakili

Distributed to the book trade worldwide by Springer Science+Business Media New York, 233 Spring Street, 6th Floor, New York, NY 10013. Phone 1-800-SPRINGER, fax (201) 348-4505, e-mail orders-ny@springer-sbm.com, or visit www.springeronline.com. Apress Media, LLC is a California LLC and the sole member (owner) is Springer Science + Business Media Finance Inc (SSBM Finance Inc). SSBM Finance Inc is a **Delaware** corporation.

For information on translations, please e-mail rights@apress.com, or visit http://www.apress.com/rights-permissions.

Apress titles may be purchased in bulk for academic, corporate, or promotional use. eBook versions and licenses are also available for most titles. For more information, reference our Print and eBook Bulk Sales web page at http://www.apress.com/bulk-sales.

Any source code or other supplementary material referenced by the author in this book is available to readers on GitHub via the book's product page, located at www.apress.com/978-1-4842-5304-5. For more detailed information, please visit http://www.apress.com/source-code.

Printed on acid-free paper

To Mum and Dad

*For recoginizing that a Space Invaders habit and a ZX81
might eventually lead somewhere in 40 years' time...*

Table of Contents

TABLE OF CONTENTS

About the Author

Mark Cunningham is the founder of Code Angel and a Computing Science teacher with over 20 years experience teaching in Scotland. Working with high school students, Mark has learned which coding concepts new coders find difficult to understand, learn, and master. He has recognized that students want to learn to code by writing programs which will motivate and engage them. His work with Code Angel has allowed him to take his teaching beyond the classroom and reach a much wider audience online. Mark is also the co-founder of Hashtag Learning who develop online resources for schools.

About the Technical Reviewer

Massimo Nardone has more than 22 years of experiences in Security, Web/Mobile Development, Cloud, and IT Architecture. His true IT passions are Security and Android.

He has been programming and teaching how to program with Android, Perl, PHP, Java, VB, Python, C/C++, and MySQL for more than 20 years.

He holds a Master of Science in Computing Science from the University of Salerno, Italy.

He has worked as a Project Manager, Software Engineer, Research Engineer, Chief Security Architect, Information Security Manager, PCI/SCADA Auditor, and Senior Lead IT Security/Cloud/SCADA Architect for many years.

His technical skills include Security, Android, Cloud, Java, MySQL, Drupal, Cobol, Perl, Web and Mobile Development, MongoDB, D3, Joomla, Couchbase, C/C++, WebGL, Python, Pro Rails, Django CMS, Jekyll, Scratch, and so on.

He currently works as Chief Information Security Officer (CISO) for Cargotec Oyj.

He worked as Visiting Lecturer and Supervisor for exercises at the Networking Laboratory of the Helsinki University of Technology (Aalto University). He holds four international patents (PKI, SIP, SAML, and Proxy areas).

Massimo has reviewed more than 40 IT books for different publishing companies, and he is the coauthor of *Pro Android Games* (Apress, 2015).

CHAPTER 1

Introduction

Welcome to Python game programming with Code Angel. In this book, you will write the Python program code required to build four amazing games, learning how to code as you go along.

The four games you will make are shown in the following.

Figure 1-1 shows the Forest Bomber game.

Figure 1-1. *Forest Bomber*

© Mark Cunningham 2020
M. Cunningham, *Game Programming with Code Angel*,
https://doi.org/10.1007/978-1-4842-5305-2_1

Figure 1-2 shows the Snapper game.

Figure 1-2. *Snapper*

Figure 1-3 shows the Alien Invasion game.

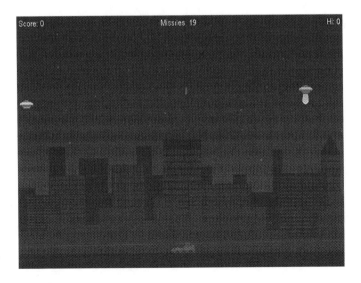

Figure 1-3. *Alien Invasion*

Figure 1-4 shows the Golf game.

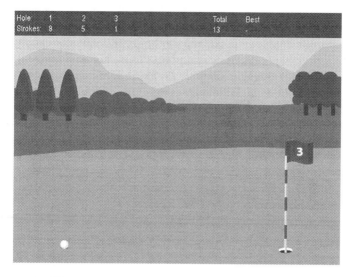

Figure 1-4. *Golf*

Coding a game

Each game is built up steadily over several chapters. Take your time working through each chapter, adding the program code as instructed. New concepts will be explained as they are introduced.

As you finish each game, you should run your program to check that it works as expected. If it doesn't, don't worry. It's quite common for a program to contain errors which are known as **bugs**. If your program has a bug, carefully compare your code with the code from this book and try to spot any differences. Missing out just one single character or typing a character in the wrong place can prevent a program from running.

Have fun playing your finished game or impress your friends by letting them play the game that you have programmed!

Python and Pygame

In order to run any of the code in this book, you will need to install the Python programming language on your computer. This is a fairly straightforward process. Follow the installation instructions on the Python web site: www.python.org.

Once you have installed Python, you need to install the Pygame library which extends Python and provides many of the functions required to make games. Visit the web site for information on how to download and install Pygame: www.pygame.org.

Both Python and Pygame are open source and completely free.

Choosing an IDE

Now that you have installed Python and Pygame, you are ready to begin coding. You are probably wondering where to actually type your Python code.

The best way to do this is by using an *IDE*. IDE stands for integrated development environment. It's what programmers use to enter, run, and debug their code.

There are lots of different IDEs to choose from. At Code Angel, we recommend one of the following IDEs to get you started. They are all free and available for Windows, MacOS, and Linux.

Python IDLE

Pros: Installed with Python, fine for small projects
   Cons: Basic, limited debugging, not great for larger projects
   Rating 3/5

Thonny

Pros: Easy to use

Cons: Not as polished as PyCharm

Rating 4/5

Windows, Mac, or Linux

PyCharm Edu

Pros: Works well for large projects

Cons: More complex interface and menu options, steep learning curve

Installation: Needs Pygame to be added under Settings ➤ Project Interpreter

Rating 5/5

Once you install whichever IDE you think best meets your needs, you are ready to start coding.

Bugs and debugging

A **bug** is simply an error in a computer program. Bugs are so called because early computers were very large and insects would get inside the system and cause a short circuit. Nowadays, a bug refers to program code which contains an error.

A bug may cause a program to crash or prevent it from working in the way that was expected. **Debugging** means finding and fixing bugs in program code.

When a program crashes, it may display an error message. Sometimes the message can be difficult to understand. The most important thing to note is the line number at which the error occurred. Find the line number in your program, and compare it very closely with the same line of code from this book. Look for any differences. Your program code must be *exactly* the same as the code from the book. Also check that the lines above and below the reported line number are correct.

A logic error is an error which causes a program to run incorrectly but does not necessarily cause the program to crash. Because there is no error message, logic errors can be difficult to find.

With logic errors, you need to work out where in the program code the error might be. For example, imagine a game where the objective is to shoot a spaceship. Each time that the player hits the spaceship, they should have ten points added to their score. However, you find when running the game that ten points are subtracted each time a spaceship is hit. This would be an example of a logic error.

This logic error must have occurred when the program updated the game score. It is likely that a minus sign has been used instead of a plus sign, and that is what has caused the error. The game will not actually crash, but the player will soon get fed up losing points every time they hit a spaceship!

Common mistakes

While bugs can be caused in many different ways, there are some common mistakes you should look out for.

Indentation

In Python, indentation levels are very important. Indentation errors can cause a program to crash or not work correctly. Each level of indentation should be either four spaces or a single tab.

```
while True:
_____for event in pygame.event.get():
_____key_pressed = pygame.key.get_pressed()
```

Make sure that you carefully check indentation levels as you enter new lines of code.

Variable and function names

Make sure variable names and function names are spelled correctly.

```
score  ✓
csore  ✗
```

Variable names and function names use underscores between words.

```
plane_exploded  ✓
```

Variable names and function names cannot contain spaces.

```
plane exploded  ✗
```

Case

Python is case sensitive. This applies to Python commands, as well as function and variable names.

So in a Python program, `score`, `Score`, and `SCORE` are three completely different things.

Brackets and quotes

Brackets and quotes come in pairs.

If there is an opening bracket, there must also be a closing bracket
( )
The same applies to quotes
" " or ' '

Missing colons

`if` statements, `for` statements, `def` function declarations, and `class` definitions all end in a colon. It's common for beginners to miss the colon out by mistake – if you are getting an error, make sure that the colon is not missing.

```
if bomb.y > SCREEN_HEIGHT:
```

Comments

A comment is a note or explanation included in the program code. In Python, comments begin with the # hash symbol and will often be displayed in a different color by the IDE.

Comments are ignored by the computer when the program is being run. All of the programs in this book include comments to help explain what the program code is doing. These comments don't affect the program and so do not actually have to be entered, but it is good practice to include them.

Time to get started...

You are now ready to start programming the games in this book, beginning with Forest Bomber. You might find coding tricky at times, you might get frustrated, but to become a programmer, the key is to stick with it and not give up. And of course...have fun!

## CHAPTER 2

Forest Bomber part 1: A first level

Dusty sunbeams cut eerie shadows across the forest floor. Dawn was breaking.

The radio message was faint at first, but became gradually stronger. 'Mayday...Mayday...' The distant hum of an airplane engine could be heard above the trees.

Captain Matt Johnson knew he was in trouble. The fuel gauge in his B-58 Hustler was well into the red, indicating that he would have no more than two minutes before his plane went down. He glanced out of the jet fighter window. Where could he land? There was nothing but a sea of trees beneath him.

He knew he had only one option remaining. Captain Johnson would have to clear a landing strip using the bombs fitted to the Hustler.

Getting started

We have an idea for a game, Forest Bomber. In Forest Bomber, an airplane is running out of fuel and has to land safely at the bottom of the screen. However, there are trees in the forest which will cause the plane to explode if it crashes into one. So the pilot of the plane – our player – has to try and bomb the trees to clear a landing strip.

OK, so we have an idea for a game, and it seems simple enough. That's a good start. Now what?

Before we even begin writing any of the Forest Bomber code, we need to design the game in more detail by taking the idea and breaking it down into smaller steps, covered here and in Chapters 3 to 5 as follows:

1. Set up game environment (Chapter 2).

2. Initialize variables (Chapter 2).

3. Display the background (Chapter 2).

4. Draw the forest (Chapter 2).

5. Draw the plane (Chapter 3).

6. Move the plane (Chapter 3).

7. Drop the bomb (Chapter 4).

8. Game over/level up (Chapter 4).

9. Display scoreboard and messages (Chapter 5).

I've split the steps over four chapters so we could gradually build up the game. The first two steps might seem a little odd, but the remaining seven steps should make some sense.

By the end of step 4, we will have designed and coded the layout for the first level of Forest Bomber.

Let's begin by sketching out how the game screen will look (Figure 2-1). The plane should start in the top left-hand area of the screen, and the forest, which the player must clear in order to land, will run along the bottom of the screen. As this will be the first level, we will start with four trees in the forest, but the number of trees will increase in each level making the game progressively more difficult.

Figure 2-1. *Forest Bomber level 1 design*

Step 1: Set up the game environment

Before we can even begin to think about planning the main gameplay, we have to start by setting up some basic elements of the game environment. This is fairly boring stuff, and so the plan is to skip by it as quickly as possible so that we can concentrate on the main game where we will be able to develop much more useful and interesting coding skills. OK, here goes. Enter the lines of code exactly as they are shown in code listing 1 in Figure 2-2.

```
1    #!/usr/bin/python
2    # Forest Bomber
3    # Code Angel
4
5    import sys
6    import os
7    import pygame
8    from pygame.locals import *
9
10   # Define the colours
11   WHITE = (255, 255, 255)
12   PURPLE = (96, 85, 154)
13   LIGHT_BLUE = (157, 220, 241)
14   DARK_BLUE = (63, 111, 182)
15   GREEN = (57, 180, 22)
16
17   # Define constants
18   SCREEN_WIDTH = 640
19   SCREEN_HEIGHT = 480
20   SCOREBOARD_MARGIN = 4
21   LINE_HEIGHT = 18
22   BOX_WIDTH = 300
23   BOX_HEIGHT = 150
24
25   TOTAL_LEVELS = 4
26   MAX_TREES = 12
27   TREE_SPACING = 40
28   FIRST_TREE = 140
29   GROUND_HEIGHT = 3
30   TREE_OFF_GROUND = 4
31
32   PLANE_START_X = 0
33   PLANE_START_Y = 54
34
```

Figure 2-2. *Forest Bomber code listing 1*

We won't worry too much about the code at this stage, but if you want to know more, the following explains what it does:

- Lines 1–3 are called comments. They are ignored by the computer.

- Lines 5–8 tell the computer that we are going to use some additional Python code which has to be imported.

- Lines 11–15 are some of the colors we will be using later in the program.

- Lines 18–32 set up some values which will be used throughout the program. For example, SCREEN_ WIDTH and SCREEN_HEIGHT will be used to draw the actual game screen at 640 × 480 pixels, TREE_SPACING will be used to keep a 40-pixel space between each of the trees, and PLANE_START_Y will be used to start the plane 54 pixels down from the top of the screen.

Again, enter the lines of code shown in code listing 2 in Figure 2-3.

```
35    # Setup
36    os.environ['SDL_VIDEO_CENTERED'] = '1'
37    pygame.mixer.pre_init(44100, -16, 2, 512)
38    pygame.mixer.init()
39    pygame.init()
40    game_screen = pygame.display.set_mode((SCREEN_WIDTH, SCREEN_HEIGHT))
41    pygame.display.set_caption('Forest Bomber')
42    clock = pygame.time.Clock()
43    font = pygame.font.SysFont('Helvetica', 16)
44
45    # Load images
46    background_image = pygame.image.load('background.png').convert()
47    tree_image = pygame.image.load('tree.png').convert_alpha()
48    burn_tree_image = pygame.image.load('burning_tree.png').convert_alpha()
49    plane_image = pygame.image.load('plane.png').convert_alpha()
50    burn_plane_image = pygame.image.load('burning_plane.png').convert_alpha()
51    bomb_image = pygame.image.load('bomb.png').convert_alpha()
52
53    # Load sounds
54    explosion_sound = pygame.mixer.Sound('explosion.ogg')
55    tree_sound = pygame.mixer.Sound('tree_explosion.ogg')
56
```

Figure 2-3. *Forest Bomber code listing 2*

- Lines 36–43 set up the window in which the game will be displayed.

- Lines 46–51 load the graphics which will be used in the game.

- Lines 54–55 load the audio files which will be used in the game.

Step 2: Initialize variables

Now that all of the boring stuff is out of the way, we can start to write the game.

Score and lives

We will begin by gaining an understanding of variables. A variable stores a piece of information or data to be used in a program. Think of a variable as being like a box. Each variable must have its own unique name.

In Forest Bomber, we need to keep track of the score. To do this, we use a variable. We will create a box (a variable), give it the name score and place the number 0 in it.

When a variable is first given a value, it is being *initialized*. The score variable is *initialized* with the value 0 (Figure 2-4).

Figure 2-4. *The variable score, which stores the value 0*

We will also need to keep track of the game level. Again, we use a variable, but this time we will call it level and initialize it with 1, because the game will begin at level 1 (Figure 2-5).

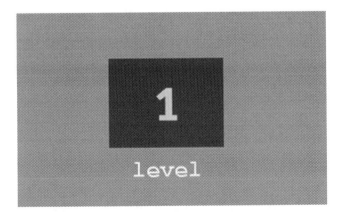

Figure 2-5. *The variable level, which stores the value 1*

Variables can store different types of data. Our score and level variables are both *integers*. An integer is a whole number which can be positive, negative, or zero.

Enter the code to initialize all of the game variables, as shown in code listing 3 in Figure 2-6.

```
# Initialise variables
level = 1
score = 0
hi_score = 0
speed_boost = 0

plane_exploded = False
level_cleared = False
plane_front = 0
plane_explode_sound_played = False


bomb_dropped = False
bomb = bomb_image.get_rect()

plane = plane_image.get_rect()
plane.x = PLANE_START_X
plane.y = PLANE_START_Y

tree = tree_image.get_rect()
tree.y = SCREEN_HEIGHT - tree.height - TREE_OFF_GROUND

burning_tree = 0
tree_timer = 0

burning_trees = []

# Set up different forests for each level
forest_1 = ['T', '-', 'T', '-', '-', '-', 'T', '-', '-', '-', '-', 'T']
forest_2 = ['-', 'T', '-', '-', 'T', '-', 'T', '-', 'T', 'T', '-', 'T']
forest_3 = ['T', 'T', '-', '-', 'T', '-', 'T', 'T', 'T', 'T', '-', '-']
forest_4 = ['T', 'T', '-', '-', 'T', 'T', 'T', '-', 'T', 'T', 'T', '-']
forest = list(forest_1)
```

Figure 2-6. *Forest Bomber code listing 3*

Line 57 initializes the level variable with the value 1.
Line 58 initializes the score variable with the value 0.

Key learning   A *variable* is like a box which can store some data or information. Each variable has its own unique name and is initialized as follows:

```
score = 0
lives = 1
```

Forest list variable

Lines 85–88 use a special type of variable to set up the tree formation for each level.

The variables forest_1, forest_2, forest_3, and forest_4 are lists. A list is a special kind of variable because it can store more than one item of data. There are four different forest lists because there will be four levels in the game.

Each forest list stores 12 items, which can be either

- 'T' which represents a tree
- '–' which represents a space

Figures 2-7 to 2-10 show how the four forests are stored as lists and how each list is then mapped to a tree drawn on the screen. We will learn later in this chapter how we actually draw the trees.

Figure 2-7. Level 1 illustration using the forest_1 list

Figure 2-8. *Level 2 illustration using the forest_2 list*

Figure 2-9. *Level 3 illustration using the forest_3 list*

Figure 2-10. *Level 4 illustration using the forest_4 list*

Notice that as we move from forest 1 through to forest 4, there are more trees. This is so that each level is harder than the one before. If you wish, you can customize Forest Bomber by changing the combination of 'T's and '-'s in the list to change the formation of trees in a level (although probably best not to do that just yet).

Key learning   A *list* is a special type of variable which can be used to store multiple items of data.

So far, we have entered almost 90 lines of code, and nothing is happening in our game yet!

Step 3: Display the background

It is time to display some of the graphics for Forest Bomber, and we will begin with the background graphic. Enter lines 91–105 as shown in code listing 4 in Figure 2-11.

```
91      # Main game loop
92      while True:
93
94          for event in pygame.event.get():
95
96              # User quits
97              if event.type == QUIT:
98                  pygame.quit()
99                  sys.exit()
100
101         # Draw background
102         game_screen.blit(background_image, [0, 0])
103
104         pygame.display.update()
105         clock.tick(30)
106
```

Figure 2-11. Forest Bomber code listing 4

Notice that line 94 and lines 102–105 are indented (which means they are spaced in from the left of the page). Also notice that line 97 has a double indent, and lines 98–99 have three levels of indentation. Python is very specific about each level of indentation. Each level of indentation should be exactly four spaces (or one tab).

Let's take a closer look at line 102.

```
game_screen.blit(background_image, [0, 0])
```

This is the line of code which draws our game background. It uses the *blit* command to display the background image in the top left-hand corner of the game window. The background image itself is 640 × 480 pixels which is exactly the same size as the Forest Bomber window, so it fits in place perfectly.

Pygame uses a coordinate system to draw graphics on screen, and the point (0,0) is in the upper left-hand corner as can be seen in Figure 2-12.

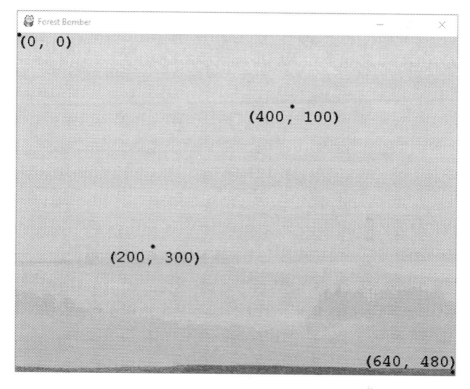

Figure 2-12. *Pygame coordinate system*

There are a couple of other things to note about the way in which the background image is displayed by line 102:

- game_screen is a variable which was initialized in line 40, and it is a representation of the Forest Bomber game window.

- background_image is a variable which was initialized in line 46. It stores the image file *background.png*.

Now it's time to test our program. Run Forest Bomber, and if you have entered the code correctly, the background image should be displayed. If you get an error, carefully check that all code has been entered correctly. Even the slightest mistake will cause the program to not run.

Key learning   `blit` draws an image onto a Pygame screen.

Pygame uses a coordinate system, where the point (0,0) is the top-left corner of the game.

Each level of indentation is four spaces or one tab.

Step 4: Draw the forest

Now that we have our game background, it's time to draw the forest.

We have already seen that the layout of the forest for each level is stored in a list. For level 1, the forest layout is held in the list `forest_1`. The next block of code will draw the forest on top of the game background.

To draw the forest, code listing 5 should be added between lines 102 and 104 as shown in Figure 2-13.

```
102     game_screen.blit(background_image, [0, 0])
103
104     pygame.display.update()


103
104     # Draw forest
105     for column, forest_item in enumerate(forest):
106         tree.x = FIRST_TREE + column * TREE_SPACING
107         if forest_item == 'T':
108             game_screen.blit(tree_image, [tree.x, tree.y])
109         elif forest_item == 'B':
110             game_screen.blit(burn_tree_image, [tree.x, tree.y])
111
```

Figure 2-13. *Forest Bomber code listing 5*

Some lines of code listing 5 in Figure 2-13 are quite complicated, and so the techniques used will be picked up later in the book.

For now, we will concentrate on lines 106–108 because they actually draw the trees in our forest.

Using math to calculate tree position

Line 106 does a bit of math to work out how far across the game screen to place each tree.

```
tree.x = FIRST_TREE + column * TREE_SPACING
```

- The variable `tree.x` will store the x coordinate of the tree (how far across the screen it should be displayed).

- `FIRST_TREE` is a variable which has already been given the value of 140 in line 28 of the program.

- `column` will be 0 to begin with but will then become 1, then 2, then 3, and all the way up to 11. This is because there can be 12 different positions at which a tree can be displayed from left to right.

- `TREE_SPACING` is also a variable which has its value assigned earlier in the code – if you check back to line 27, you will see it was set to 40. This variable is the number of pixels between each tree in the forest.

- The $*$ sign in Python means multiply.

So let's do the math...

```
When column is 0:
tree.x = FIRST_TREE + column * TREE_SPACING
       = 140 + 0 * 40
       = 140

When column is 1:
tree.x = FIRST_TREE + column * TREE_SPACING
       = 140 + 1 * 40
       = 180
```

21

```
When column is 2:
tree.x = FIRST_TREE + column * TREE_SPACING
       = 140 + 2 * 40
       = 220
```

And so on. This is how we work out the x coordinate of each of the 12 trees.

Deciding which trees to draw

But wait – we don't actually want to display all 12 trees. We only want to display a tree when our forest list has a T. That's where line 107 comes in.

```
if forest_item == 'T':
```

This is an if statement. if statements are used in programming to make a decision.

This code is saying

- Only draw a tree if the forest_item is equal to 'T'.

Notice the use of the double equals (==) in line 107. In Python, we use == to check if two things are equal.

Line 107 doesn't actually draw anything though; it is only making the decision. If the forest_item is equal to 'T', then line 108 will be executed, and line 108 is the line which draws the tree on the screen.

```
if forest_item == 'T':
    game_screen.blit(tree_image, [tree.x, tree.y])
```

Notice that line 108 is indented. If the forest_item is a 'T', then all indented lines directly below the line will be executed. In this case, the only indented line is 108, so that will be executed if the forest_item is a 'T'.

Line 108 uses the blit command to draw a tree_image onto the game_screen at coordinates (tree.x,tree.y). But where do all of these commands and values come from?

- We learned about blit earlier in this chapter when we drew the background image.

- We also saw that game_screen is a variable which stores the Forest Bomber game window.

- tree_image is a variable used to store the image of a tree. It was initialized in line 47 of the program where it was loaded with the file *tree.png* – the picture of a tree.

- We have already seen how tree.x is initialized by some math which calculates how far horizontally across the screen each tree should be placed.

- tree.y is a variable initialized in line 77 of the program. It uses some math to work out where to place the tree vertically, a few pixels above the bottom of the game screen.

Let's ignore lines 109–110. They will display the image of a tree on fire if it has been hit by a bomb. As we have not written the code to drop a bomb yet, these lines won't actually do anything.

We can summarize lines 105–108 as follows:

- Go through each forest item in our forest list.

- Use math to calculate the x coordinate of the tree.

- If the forest item is a tree, then draw a tree in the correct location.

Run the program. The four trees of Forest Bomber level 1 should be displayed along the bottom of the game window.

Key learning   if is used to make a decision.

Double equals (==) are used to check if two things are equal.

The indented lines below an if statement will be executed if the statement works out to be true.

Summary

Phew! No one said learning to code would be easy. We have covered a lot of complex programming in this first chapter because we prefer to dive right in. Don't worry if it all seems difficult to understand. It is, but it will get easier, and we will revisit many of these topics as we work through the book.

So far, we have written lots of lines of code, and all we have to show for it is our game background and some trees. The Forest Bomber game will begin to take a bit more shape in the next chapter.

CHAPTER 3

Forest Bomber part 2: Is it a bird…?

Captain Matt Johnson looked out of the window of his B-58 Hustler. The forest below stretched out like a giant green carpet as far as the eye could see. He studied the fuel gauge again. The dial pointed directly at the letter E.

Empty.

The B-58 Hustler began making its descent…

In the previous chapter, we completed steps 1–4 of our game design and learned how to draw the background and trees onto the screen. In this chapter, we will learn how to draw and move Captain Johnson's B-58 Hustler plane.

Picking up the steps from our original plan

5. Draw the plane.

6. Move the plane.

Step 5: Draw the plane

Insert code listing 6 between lines 112 and 117 as shown in Figure 3-1.

© Mark Cunningham 2020
M. Cunningham, *Game Programming with Code Angel*,
https://doi.org/10.1007/978-1-4842-5305-2_3

```
103
104     # Draw forest
105     for column, forest_item in enumerate(forest):
106         tree.x = FIRST_TREE + column * TREE_SPACING
107         if forest_item == 'T':
108             game_screen.blit(tree_image, [tree.x, tree.y])
109         elif forest_item == 'B':
110             game_screen.blit(burn_tree_image, [tree.x, tree.y])
111
112     # Draw plane
113     if plane_exploded is False:
114         game_screen.blit(plane_image, [plane.x, plane.y])
115     else:
116         plane.y = SCREEN_HEIGHT - burn_plane_image.get_height() - TREE_OFF_GROUND
117         game_screen.blit(burn_plane_image, [plane.x, plane.y])
118
119     pygame.display.update()
120     clock.tick(30)
```

Figure 3-1. *Forest Bomber code listing 6*

Let's take a closer look at lines 113 and 114 in Figure 3-2.

```
if plane_exploded is False:
    game_screen.blit(plane_image, [plane.x, plane.y])
```

Figure 3-2. *Forest Bomber code listing lines 113 and 114*

We can see another if statement has been used here, so we know that the program code is making a decision. It is checking to see if plane_ exploded is False. If we look all the way back to line 63, we can see that plane_exploded is a variable and it is initialized to False.

What is False? In programming, there is a variable type known as a Boolean, and it can have one of only two possible values: True or False. Boolean variables are useful in game programming, because they can only be one or the other. There is no in-between. They can only be either True or False. Later in the program, we will set the value of the plane_exploded Boolean variable to True when our plane crashes into a tree. But for now, it's False.

Given that the value of plane_exploded is False (at least for now), then line 114 will execute. Line 114 uses the blit command to draw the plane image at coordinates (plane.x,plane.y).

We can see from previous lines of code in our program that

- plane_image is a variable which stores *plane.png* (line 45).

- plane.x is initialized with the value PLANE_START_X (line 73). PLANE_START_X is initialized with the value 0 (line 32) so plane.x will have the value 0.

- plane.y is initialized with the value PLANE_START_Y (line 74). PLANE_START_Y is initialized with the value 54 (line 33) so plane.y will have the value 54.

Our plane will first appear at coordinates (0,54).

Run the program. The plane should appear near the top of the screen, on the far left-hand side.

Key learning   A Boolean variable can store one of two values: True or False.

Step 6: Move the plane

In game programming, we move a sprite around the game screen by changing its coordinates and then redrawing the screen.

Fly across the screen

In order to get the plane to move across the screen, we increase the x coordinate and then redraw the screen. The more we increase the x coordinate by, the faster the plane will fly. We will increase the x coordinate by 5, which means it will move to the right by 5 pixels.

Insert code listing 7 at line 101.

```
91      # Main game loop
92      while True:
93
94          for event in pygame.event.get():
95
96              # User quits
97              if event.type == QUIT:
98                  pygame.quit()
99                  sys.exit()
100
101          # Update plane location
102          plane.x = plane.x + 5
103
104          # Draw background
105          game_screen.blit(background_image, [0, 0])
```

Figure 3-3. *Forest Bomber code listing 7*

Line 101 can be read as

- Take the variable which stores the plane's x coordinate.

- Add 5 onto it.

We learned earlier in this chapter that `plane.x` was initialized with 0. When line 101 is executed, it will take what is stored in `plane.x` (in this case 0) and add on 5. So the new value of `plane.x` is 5.

We need to do this repeatedly; otherwise, the plane will only move 5 pixels once, which won't be much use. It's time to look back at another line of code that we wrote earlier, line 92.

```
while True:
```

Figure 3-4. *Forest Bomber code listing line 92*

`while True` means to repeat doing something – forever. Look down at the rest of the program code below line 92. It is all indented. This means that all the indented code will keep repeating, forever (well at least until the user closes the game window). This also means that 5 will be repeatedly added onto the x coordinate of the plane.

In order to see the plane actually move, we need to redraw the screen. Let's look at some code that we wrote earlier but didn't pay much attention to, the last two lines of code in the program, lines 122 and 123.

```
pygame.display.update()
clock.tick(30)
```

Figure 3-5. *Forest Bomber code listing lines 122 and 123*

Line 122 redraws the screen, while line 123 determines how many times the screen should be redrawn in one second, in this case 30.

So our program now draws the plane, moves it 5 pixels right, redraws the plane, moves it another 5 pixels right, and so on, creating the illusion of the plane moving.

Test this by running the program.

Fantastic, right? Except for one thing. Our plane flies off the end of the screen never to be seen again, and that won't make for much of a game!

Fly down the screen

Let's take a moment to consider the logic to make the plane fly down the screen:

- If the plane flies off the right-hand side of the screen, move it down the screen and back to the left-hand side.

To move the plane

- Down: We add 100 to its y coordinate.

- Back to the left: We set its x coordinate back to 0.

Add the code to fly the plane down the screen shown in code listing 8, Figure 3-6.

```
# Update plane location
plane.x = plane.x + 5

if plane.x >= SCREEN_WIDTH:
    plane.x = 0
    plane.y += 100

# Draw background
game_screen.blit(background_image, [0, 0])
```

Figure 3-6. *Forest Bomber code listing 8*

Run the program. Now the plane should fly to the right edge of the screen and then drop down by 100 pixels beginning again on the left-hand side, except now it flies all the way to the bottom of the screen and then disappears. We will fix this in a later chapter.

Now we are going to make a couple of minor changes to the code that flies our plane and which will be useful later.

First, adapt line 102 so that it reads as in Figure 3-7.

```
plane.x = plane.x + 5 + speed_boost
```

Figure 3-7. *Forest Bomber code listing line 102*

We have added + `speed_boost` to the end of the line, but why? We want to make the game get a little harder for levels 3 and 4. For levels 1 and 2, `speed_boost` is 0, so it makes no difference to the speed of the plane. But for levels 3 and 4, we will set `speed_boost` to 1. This means we will be adding 6 to the plane's x coordinate for levels 3 and 4 instead of 5. It will make the plane fly slightly faster across the screen and make the game just that little bit harder.

The second change is to insert an `if` statement at line 102, Figure 3-8.

```
if level_cleared is False and plane_exploded is False:
```

Figure 3-8. *Forest Bomber code listing line 102 with* `if` *statement*

The purpose of this line is to make sure we only move the plane if

- We have not reached the end of the level.
- The plane has not exploded.

If either of these events occurs, we do not want to move our plane. We will learn later in the book how we change the values of `level_cleared` when the level is over and `plane_exploded` when the plane crashes into a tree.

The code should now look like code listing 9 in Figure 3-9. One very important thing to note – because we added an if statement at line 102, lines 103, 105, 106, and 107 have all had one extra indentation.

```
96    # User quits
97    if event.type == QUIT:
98        pygame.quit()
99        sys.exit()
100
101   # Update plane location
102   if level_cleared is False and plane_exploded is False:
103       plane.x = plane.x + 5 + speed_boost
104
105       if plane.x >= SCREEN_WIDTH:
106           plane.x = 0
107           plane.y += 100
108
109   # Draw background
110   game_screen.blit(background_image, (0, 0))
111
```

Figure 3-9. *Forest Bomber code listing 9*

Key learning   To move a sprite, change its coordinates and then redraw the screen.

while True is used in Python game programming to repeat forever.

CHAPTER 4

Forest Bomber part 3: Bombs away...

Captain Johnson looked down at the flight control panel of his B-58 Hustler jet. He knew what he had to do. His finger hovered over the button marked 'Release.' Timing was all-important now. He could not afford to miss his target. A bead of sweat slipped slowly down his right temple.

Wait...Wait...Wait...Now!

He hit the button, and a bomb dropped out of the B-58 and began hurtling toward the forest below.

In the last chapter, we learned how to make the plane fly across the screen. Next, we will learn how to write the code which will drop a bomb, and then we will develop the end of level and game over code.

From our plan

7. Drop the bomb.

8. Game over/level up.

© Mark Cunningham 2020
M. Cunningham, *Game Programming with Code Angel*,
https://doi.org/10.1007/978-1-4842-5305-2_4

Step 7: Drop the bomb

Key presses

So far in Forest Bomber, there is not much for the player to do other than sit back and watch the plane fly across and down the screen until it eventually disappears off the bottom right-hand corner. Not much of a game! We want our player to be able to interact with Forest Bomber so that when they hit the spacebar, a bomb is dropped.

Pygame has a way of capturing or storing any key presses.

The code will look as in Figure 4-1.

```
key_pressed = pygame.key.get_pressed()
if key_pressed[pygame.K_SPACE]:
```

Figure 4-1. *Key press code*

- The first line assigns any key presses to a variable key_pressed.

- The second line checks to see if the key_pressed variable holds a specific key, in this case the spacebar.

Let's build the key press code into Forest Bomber. Insert code listing 10 (Figure 4-2) at line 96.

```
94    for event in pygame.event.get():
95
96        # Space key pressed, drop bomb
97        key_pressed = pygame.key.get_pressed()
98        if key_pressed[pygame.K_SPACE]:
99            if bomb_dropped is False and level_cleared is False and plane_exploded is False:
100               bomb_dropped = True
101               bomb.x = plane.x + 15
102               bomb.y = plane.y + 10
103
104       # User quits
105       if event.type == QUIT:
106           pygame.quit()
107           sys.exit()
```

Figure 4-2. *Forest Bomber code listing 10*

We already know that lines 97 and 98 check to see if the spacebar was pressed. Lines 99–102 is the code which will run when the spacebar is pressed.

Let's examine line 99 more closely. It is another `if` statement. This statement checks for three things. It checks if

- `bomb_dropped is False`

- `level_cleared is False`

- `plane_exploded is False`

In Chapter 3, we learned about Boolean variables that can store either `True` or `False`. Let's look again at the `if` statement to work out exactly what we are checking for:

- `bomb_dropped is False`

  Is there a bomb already dropping? If so, we do not want to allow another bomb to be dropped because it would make the game too easy. We have to wait until any previous bombs have exploded or disappear off-screen before allowing the player to drop the next one.

- `level_cleared is False`

  We can't drop a bomb if the level has cleared because the game is waiting to level up.

- `plane_exploded is False`

  We can't drop a bomb if the plane has exploded because it is game over.

We need all three of these statements to be `False` before we can drop a bomb. To check that they are all `False`, we place **and** between each statement.

If all three statements are False, then lines 100 and 102 are executed:

- Line 100 sets the Boolean variable bomb_dropped to True. This will prevent another bomb being dropped until bomb_dropped is set back to False again.

- Line 101 sets the x coordinate of the bomb to the value of the x coordinate of the plane, plus 15. This means that the bomb will be displayed horizontally in the middle of the plane.

- Line 102 sets the y coordinate of the bomb to the value of the y coordinate of the plane plus 10. This means that the bomb will be displayed 10 pixels below the plane.

We now need some code to display the bomb on screen. Remember how we wrote the code to display the plane by using the blit command? We will use very similar code to display the bomb.

Insert code listing 11 (Figure 4-3) at line 135.

```
128        # Draw plane
129        if plane_exploded is False:
130            game_screen.blit(plane_image, (plane.x, plane.y))
131        else:
132            plane.y = SCREEN_HEIGHT - burn_plane_image.get_height() - TREE_OFF_GROUND
133            game_screen.blit(burn_plane_image, (plane.x, plane.y))
134
135        # Draw bomb
136        if bomb_dropped is True:
137            game_screen.blit(bomb_image, (bomb.x, bomb.y))
138
139        pygame.display.update()
140        clock.tick(30)
```

Figure 4-3. Forest Bomber code listing 11

Key learning `pygame.key.get_pressed()` checks any key presses.

The and keyword can be used to join multiple conditions within a single `if` statement.

When and is used, all the statements have to work out as being true for the `if` statement to execute.

Now run the program and try hitting the spacebar. A bomb should appear where the plane is – it just doesn't move yet.

Move the bomb

In Chapter 3, we learned how to move the plane by changing its coordinates and then redrawing the screen. We will move the bomb in exactly the same way.

Add code listing 12 (Figure 4-4) at line 117.

```
113        if plane.x >= SCREEN_WIDTH:
114            plane.x = 0
115            plane.y += 100
116
117        # Update bomb location
118        if bomb_dropped is True:
119            bomb.y += 5
120            bomb.x += 3
121
122        # Draw background
123        game_screen.blit(background_image, [0, 0])
```

Figure 4-4. *Forest Bomber code listing 12*

This code can be read as

- If a bomb has been dropped

- Move it down 3 pixels.

- Move it right 5 pixels.

Test the game by running it. If we press the spacebar, the bomb drops. The only problem is it keeps going off the screen and we can never launch another bomb. This is because the bomb_dropped Boolean variable is set to True when the bomb is launched and never changed back to False.

Remember the code that tests if a bomb can be dropped (Figure 4-5)?

```
if key_pressed[pygame.K_SPACE]:
    if bomb_dropped is False and level_cleared is False and plane_exploded is False:
```

Figure 4-5. *Code which tests if a bomb can be launched*

A bomb can only be launched if bomb_dropped is False. Let's fix our program so that when a bomb disappears off-screen, bomb_dropped is reset to False. Insert code listing 13 (Figure 4-6) at line 122 (note that line 122 has two indentations – eight spaces).

```
117         # Update bomb location
118         if bomb_dropped is True:
119             bomb.y += 5
120             bomb.x += 3
121
122             if bomb.y > SCREEN_HEIGHT:
123                 bomb_dropped = False
124
125             if bomb.x > SCREEN_WIDTH:
126                 bomb_dropped = False
127
128         # Draw background
129         game_screen.blit(background_image, [0, 0])
```

Figure 4-6. *Forest Bomber code listing 13*

- Line 122 tests to see if the bomb has gone below the bottom of the screen.

- Line 125 tests to see if the bomb has gone beyond the right-hand side of the screen.

If the bomb has disappeared off the bottom, or off the right of the screen, bomb_dropped will be set to False which means we can now use the spacebar to drop a new bomb.

Let's take a closer look at line 122. It compares the y coordinate of the bomb (bomb.y) with the SCREEN_HEIGHT. But how does the program know what SCREEN_HEIGHT is?

Look back to lines 18 and 19 of the program. SCREEN_WIDTH is set to 640 and SCREEN_HEIGHT is set to 480. We don't have to do this, but it makes our code easier to read. And if we decided we wanted a bigger screen for our game, say 800 × 600, then we would just have to set SCREEN_WIDTH and SCREEN_HEIGHT to 800 and 600, respectively, at the start of the program.

You may be also wondering why we use capital letters for some variable names, like SCREEN_WIDTH and SCREEN_HEIGHT. This is because they are constants. A constant is assigned a value at the start of the program, and it doesn't change. Python's naming convention suggests we should use capital letters to indicate the use of constants. That way we know that we are dealing with a constant value, and therefore its value should not be changed by the program.

There is one other part of line 122 that merits a closer look. Previously when comparing values, we have used the double equals sign (==) to check whether two values are equal. In line 122 (and also in line 125), we use the greater than (>) symbol. So line 122 actually reads

> if the y coordinate of the bomb *is greater than* the
> screen width

The full list of Python's comparison operators is as follows:

Comparison Operator	Meaning
==	Is equal to
>	Is greater than
>=	Is greater than or equal to
<	Is less than
<=	Is less than or equal to
!=	Is not equal to

Key learning   The Python naming convention suggests using capital letters to indicate a constant value.

Python has a range of comparison operators: ==, >, >=, <, <=, and !=.

Run the program to test that a new bomb can be dropped once the previous bomb has disappeared off the edge of the screen.

Exploding trees

The code to blow up a tree is quite complex, and given we are only just beginning to learn how to code, we will only focus on a small part of it. Let's begin by adding code listing 14 (Figure 4-7) at line 128.

```python
if bomb.x > SCREEN_WIDTH:
    bomb_dropped = False

# Check if bomb has hit a tree
for column, forest_item in enumerate(forest):
    if forest_item == 'T':
        tree.x = FIRST_TREE + column * TREE_SPACING

        if bomb.colliderect(tree):
            forest[column] = 'B'
            bomb_dropped = False
            burning_trees.append(column)
            tree_timer = 10
            score += 10 * level
            tree_sound.play()

# Update burning trees tree status
if tree_timer > 0:
    tree_timer -= 1
    if tree_timer == 0:
        for column in burning_trees:
            forest[column] = ' '
        del burning_trees[:]

# Draw background
game_screen.blit(background_image, (0, 0))
```

Figure 4-7.   Forest Bomber code listing 14

Let's take a brief overview of lines 128–139 to see what they do:

- Check each of the trees in the forest to see if the bomb has hit it.

- If it has

  - We increase the score.

  - We play an explosion sound.

  - We set a timer to keep a burning tree graphic on screen for ten frames.

Let's take a moment to focus on two of the more straightforward lines of code that have been used in this block, the code that is run when a bomb has hit a tree:

- Line 135 sets the Boolean variable bomb_dropped to False. This means that a new bomb can be dropped when the player hits the spacebar.

- Line 138 increases the value held in the score variable. If you remember back to the beginning of Chapter 2, we set score to 0 and level to 1. Line 138 adds 10 × the current level to score:

  - As level is currently 1, the value 10 (10 × 1) will be added to the current score.

  - As score was initialized with the value 0, score will become 10 when a first tree is hit.

  - When a second tree is hit, score will become 20 and so on.

41

We will learn how to display the score and level in the next chapter.

The code between lines 142 and 147 uses a timer to display the burning tree image for a series of ten frames before removing it from the game altogether. The code is beyond the scope of this chapter, so we will skip past it.

Test the game again. You should find that if the bomb hits a tree, it explodes.

Ground level

Our game of Forest Bomber is starting to take shape. The big problem now is that when our plane reaches the ground level, it flies through the trees and off the screen.

Code listing 15 (Figure 4-8) addresses this. Insert the code at line 149.

```
141    # Update burning trees tree status
142    if tree_timer > 0:
143        tree_timer -= 1
144        if tree_timer == 0:
145            for column in burning_trees:
146                forest[column] = '-'
147            del burning_trees[:]
148
149    # Plane on ground level
150    if plane.y >= SCREEN_HEIGHT - plane.height - GROUND_HEIGHT:
151        plane_front = plane.x + plane.width
152
153        # Edge of the screen reached so level cleared
154        if plane_front >= SCREEN_WIDTH:
155            level_cleared = True
156
157        # Check to see if plane has collided with a tree
158        else:
159            for column, forest_item in enumerate(forest):
160                if forest_item == 'T' or forest_item == 'B':
161                    tree_left = FIRST_TREE + column * TREE_SPACING
162                    if plane_front >= tree_left:
163                        plane_exploded = True
164
165    # Draw background
166    game_screen.blit(background_image, [0, 0])
```

Figure 4-8. *Forest Bomber code listing 15*

We won't go into this code in too much detail, but in summary

- Line 150 uses a bit of math to work out if the y coordinate of the plane is at the ground level.

- If it is, line 151 calculates the position of the front of the plane.

- Line 152 says if the plane has got beyond the right-hand side of the screen, then the level has been cleared, so set the Boolean variable level_cleared to True.

- Lines 158–163 check to see if the plane has hit a tree and, if it has, then set the Boolean variable plane_exploded to True.

Test the game. Now the plane will come to a halt if the player manages to clear all of the trees from the forest, or it will explode if it hits a tree.

Step 8: Game over/level up

If the plane hits a tree, then it is game over.

If the plane reaches the right-hand side of the screen on the ground level, then the game needs to move on to the next level.

In either case, we will display a message to the user to tell them what has happened and invite them to hit the return key to continue.

There are two Boolean variables which will have been set depending on what has happened previously:

- plane_exploded will have been set to True if the plane has hit a tree.

- level_cleared will have been set to True if the player has cleared all of the trees from the forest.

We will use these variables to determine what to do next.

Add code listing 16 (Figure 4-9) at line 104.

```
96       # Space key pressed, drop bomb
97       key_pressed = pygame.key.get_pressed()
98       if key_pressed[pygame.K_SPACE]:
99           if bomb_dropped is False and level_cleared is False and plane_exploded is False:
100              bomb_dropped = True
101              bomb.x = plane.x + 15
102              bomb.y = plane.y + 10
103
104      # Return key at end of game / level pressed
105      elif key_pressed[pygame.K_RETURN]:
106
107          # Plane has exploded or all levels completed - so go back to start
108          if plane_exploded is True or (level == TOTAL_LEVELS and level_cleared is True):
109              plane_exploded = False
110              plane_explode_sound_played = False
111              score = 0
112              speed_boost = 0
113              level = 1
114              forest = list(forest_1)
115              plane.x = PLANE_START_X
116              plane.y = PLANE_START_Y
117              level_cleared = False
118
119      # User quits
120      if event.type == QUIT:
121          pygame.quit()
122          sys.exit()
```

Figure 4-9. *Forest Bomber code listing 16*

Notice the use of the keyword elif at line 105 (Figure 4-10).

```
elif key_pressed[pygame.K_RETURN]:
```

Figure 4-10. *Forest Bomber code listing line 105*

It is short for *else if* and goes with the if statement at line 98. Together, these lines can be read as

> if the spacebar is pressed
>
> *drop a bomb*
>
> else if the return key is pressed
>
> *start a new level/game*

Also notice that the way in which we test if the return key is pressed is just the same as the way in which we tested if the space key was pressed.

Looking at the first part of line 108 (Figure 4-11), we are checking to see if the plane has exploded.

```
if plane_exploded is True
```

Figure 4-11. *Forest Bomber code listing line 108 (first part)*

If the plane has exploded, then we know it's game over. Lines 109–117
reset all the variables back to their start-of-game values.

There is a second part to line 108 (Figure 4-12).

```
or (level == TOTAL_LEVELS and level_cleared is True):
```

Figure 4-12. *Forest Bomber code listing line 108 (second part)*

This checks to see if we have cleared the level and also if the current
level is equal to TOTAL_LEVELS, which is 4. In other words, if we have cleared
level 4, we go back to the beginning of the game and start again at level 1.

Now that we have dealt with the game over functionality, let's add the
functionality to move up a level. Add code listing 17 (Figure 4-13) at line 119
(making sure to check the indentation very carefully).

```
107     # Plane has exploded or all levels completed - so go back to start
108     if plane_exploded is True or (level == TOTAL_LEVELS and level_cleared is True):
109         plane_exploded = False
110         plane_explode_sound_played = False
111         score = 0
112         speed_boost = 0
113         level = 1
114         forest = list(forest_1)
115         plane.x = PLANE_START_X
116         plane.y = PLANE_START_Y
117         level_cleared = False
118
119     # Level cleared - go up 1 level and load a new forest
120     elif level_cleared is True:
121         level += 1
122         level_cleared = False
123
124         if level == 2:
125             forest = list(forest_2)
126         elif level == 3:
127             forest = list(forest_3)
128             speed_boost = 1
129         else:
130             forest = list(forest_4)
131             speed_boost = 1
132
133         plane.x = PLANE_START_X
134         plane.y = PLANE_START_Y
135
136     # User quits
137     if event.type == QUIT:
138         pygame.quit()
139         sys.exit()
```

Figure 4-13. *Forest Bomber code listing 17*

Line 120 is another `elif` statement, this time paired with the `if` statement at line 108. Together they can be read like this:

if the plane has exploded and it's game over

restart the game

else if level has been cleared

level up

Let's take a closer look at some of the code used to level up (Figures 4-14, 4-15 and 4-16).

```
elif level_cleared is True:
```

Figure 4-14. *Forest Bomber code listing line 120*

- Line 120 checks to see if the level has been cleared. If it has

- Line 121 adds 1 onto the `level` variable.

```
level += 1
```

Figure 4-15. *Forest Bomber code listing line 121*

- Line 122 sets the `level_cleared` to `False` so that the game can start the next level.

```
level_cleared = False
```

Figure 4-16. *Forest Bomber code listing line 122*

- Lines 124–131 load the forest for the new level into the `forest` variable. Also note that the `speed_boost` variable is set to 1 for levels 3 and 4 to make the plane fly faster, as discussed in Chapter 3.

- Finally, lines 133 and 134 reset the x and y coordinates of the plane so that it restarts at the top left of the game screen.

Key learning   The elif statement is used along with an if statement and means else if.

To add a value onto a variable, use +=.

Now test the game:

- When the plane crashes, the user can press the return key to begin a new game.

- When all the trees are cleared, the user can press return to move onto the next level.

All that's missing now is a scoreboard and some feedback for the user at the end of each level and the end of the game.

CHAPTER 5

Forest Bomber part 4: Wrapping it up

The B-58 Hustler was now flying so low that its wings were clipping the treetops. Captain Johnson surveyed the scene. He had managed to clear an area of the forest, but it wasn't quite enough to let him land the jet safely. He would have destroyed one last tree.

Johnson knew his training had prepared him well for this moment. It would require precision and timing to release the Hustler payload at the right time. He drew his breath and hit the button marked 'Release' one final time.

The target below him exploded into a fiery ball of flame.

Seconds later, the Hustler was touching down on the ground. Captain Matt Johnson breathed a sigh of relief.

Until the next time...

Our Forest Bomber game is almost finished. The gameplay elements are all in place, and so all that is required is a scoreboard and some feedback to the user at the end of each level or when it is game over.

© Mark Cunningham 2020
M. Cunningham, *Game Programming with Code Angel*,
https://doi.org/10.1007/978-1-4842-5305-2_5

Step 9: Display scoreboard and messages

The scoreboard (Figure 5-1) will appear along the top of the game screen and display the

- Score

- Level

- High score

Figure 5-1. *Forest Bomber scoreboard*

Scoreboard background

Let's begin by drawing a solid background for our scoreboard area. We will keep the color the same light blue as the sky. Add code listing 18 at line 219.

```
215         # Draw bomb
216         if bomb_dropped is True:
217             game_screen.blit(bomb_image, [bomb.x, bomb.y])
218
219         # Display scoreboard - score, level, high score
220         scoreboard_background_rect = (0, 0, SCREEN_WIDTH, LINE_HEIGHT + 2 * SCOREBOARD_MARGIN)
221         pygame.draw.rect(game_screen, LIGHT_BLUE, scoreboard_background_rect)
222
223         pygame.display.update()
224         clock.tick(30)
```

Figure 5-2. *Forest Bomber code listing 18*

There are only two lines of code here, but they do quite a lot.

Line 220 creates the rectangle dimensions for our scoreboard background. We will use a variable to store this shape – `scoreboard_background_rect`.

To draw a rectangle, we need four pieces of information:

- The number of pixels from the left of the screen to the left of the rectangle

- The number of pixels from the top of the screen to the top of the rectangle

- The width of the rectangle

- The height of the rectangle

For our scoreboard rectangle, we will use the following values:

- Left: 0 to begin at the left-hand side of the screen

- Top: 0 to begin at the top of the screen

- Width: SCREEN_WIDTH (remember this is a constant which stores the width of the screen, 640)

- Height: LINE_HEIGHT (which is initialized to 18 at the start of the program) and SCOREBOARD_MARGIN (which is initialized to 4 at the start of the program). The actual height of the scoreboard will be LINE HEIGHT + 2 × SCOREBOARD_MARGIN, which is 26.

Line 221 draws the rectangle using the Pygame draw.rect command. It requires three pieces of information to draw the rectangle:

- The surface to draw on, in our case the game window variable game_screen.

- The color of the rectangle. Here we use the constant LIGHT_BLUE, one of the colors we initialized at the start of the program.

- The dimensions of the rectangle, which are held in the variable scoreboard_background_rect set up in line 220.

Key learning   To draw a rectangle, we need four pieces of information: left, top, width, and height.

The Pygame `draw.rect` command can be used to draw a rectangle.

Display the score

We want to display the game score in the top left-hand corner of the screen. Add code listing 19 at line 223.

```
219    # Display scoreboard - score, level, high score
220    scoreboard_background_rect = (0, 0, SCREEN_WIDTH, LINE_HEIGHT + 2 * SCOREBOARD_MARGIN)
221    pygame.draw.rect(game_screen, LIGHT_BLUE, scoreboard_background_rect)
222
223    score_text = 'Score: ' + str(score)
224    text = font.render(score_text, True, PURPLE)
225    game_screen.blit(text, (SCOREBOARD_MARGIN, SCOREBOARD_MARGIN))
226
227    pygame.display.update()
228    clock.tick(30)
```

Figure 5-3.   Forest Bomber code listing 19

Line 223 initializes the variable `score_text`. Let's look at what `score_text` will store:

- The text 'Score: '

  In computer programming, we call any sequence of characters a ***string***. So 'Score: ' is a string.

- The variable `score`

  We want to join the value stored in the variable `score` onto the end of the string 'Score: '. In order to do this, we need to convert the number held in score to a string. The Python `str` function converts a number to a string so that it can be joined onto other strings. We will learn more about the meaning of the term ***function*** in later chapters.

Let's use an example to illustrate how this works. If score is 120, score_text would be a string variable and would have the value 'Score: 120'. Note that we show strings within quote marks, but when the program is run, the quotes would not be displayed.

Line 224 takes our score_text variable and uses the Pygame font.render command to convert it to a format than can be displayed on a Pygame surface. The font will be rendered in one of our previously initialized colors, PURPLE.

Line 225 uses the blit command to display the rendered text on the game screen. It displays the text at the coordinates (SCOREBOARD_MARGIN,SCOREBOARD_MARGIN). We have already seen that SCOREBOARD_MARGIN was initialized to 4 at line 20 of the program, so our text will be displayed at the top-left corner of the screen but with a 4-pixel padding.

Key learning   A sequence of characters is called a string.

str function must be used to join a numeric value onto a string.

The Pygame font.render command is used to display text in Pygame.

Run the program, and you should see the score appearing in the top left-hand corner of the screen.

Display the level

It would be useful if Forest Bomber could display the current level of the game. We will add four lines of code to display the level in the center of the scoreboard.

Add code listing 20 at line 227.

```
223    score_text = 'Score: ' + str(score)
224    text = font.render(score_text, True, PURPLE)
225    game_screen.blit(text, (SCOREBOARD_MARGIN, SCOREBOARD_MARGIN))
226
227    level_text = 'Level: ' + str(level)
228    text = font.render(level_text, True, PURPLE)
229    text_rect = text.get_rect()
230    game_screen.blit(text, ((SCREEN_WIDTH - text_rect.width) / 2, SCOREBOARD_MARGIN))
231
232    pygame.display.update()
233    clock.tick(30)
```

Figure 5-4. Forest Bomber code listing 20

This code is very similar to the code which we used to display the score. The main difference is the way in which we center the text. To center a block of text in Pygame, we need to

- Calculate the width of the rendered rectangle which is holding the text.

- Subtract the width of the text rectangle from the overall screen width and divide by 2.

This will give is the point at which to place our rendered text so that it is perfectly centered.

Display the high score

We don't actually have any code to handle the high score yet, other than initializing the variable hi_score to 0 in line 60 of the program.

The logic which calculates the high score is actually fairly simple:

- If during the game the score goes above the previous highest score, then the new high score should become the score.

Add code listing 21 at line 197 to handle the high score logic.

```
181    # Plane on ground level
182    if plane.y >= SCREEN_HEIGHT - plane.height - GROUND_HEIGHT:
183        plane_front = plane.x + plane.width
184
185        # Edge of the screen reached so level cleared
186        if plane_front >= SCREEN_WIDTH:
187            level_cleared = True
188
189        # Check to see if plane has collided with a tree
190        else:
191            for column, forest_item in enumerate(forest):
192                if forest_item == 'T' or forest_item == 'B':
193                    tree_left = FIRST_TREE + column * TREE_SPACING
194                    if plane_front >= tree_left:
195                        plane_exploded = True
196
197    # If score is greater than high score, then new high score
198    if score > hi_score:
199        hi_score = score
200
201    # Draw background
202    game_screen.blit(background_image, (0, 0))
```

Figure 5-5. *Forest Bomber code listing 21*

Next, add code listing 22 at line 231 to display the high score at the upper right of the scoreboard.

```
227    score_text = 'Score: ' + str(score)
228    text = font.render(score_text, True, PURPLE)
229    game_screen.blit(text, [SCOREBOARD_MARGIN, SCOREBOARD_MARGIN])
230
231    hi_text = 'Hi Score: ' + str(hi_score)
232    text = font.render(hi_text, True, PURPLE)
233    text_rect = text.get_rect()
234    game_screen.blit(text, [SCREEN_WIDTH - text_rect.width - SCOREBOARD_MARGIN, SCOREBOARD_MARGIN])
235
236    level_text = 'Level: ' + str(level)
237    text = font.render(level_text, True, PURPLE)
238    text_rect = text.get_rect()
239    game_screen.blit(text, [(SCREEN_WIDTH - text_rect.width) / 2, SCOREBOARD_MARGIN])
```

Figure 5-6. *Forest Bomber code listing 22*

Run the game – we now have a fully functioning scoreboard located along the top of the screen.

Display messages

Our final task is to display some messages at the end of the game or when the level has been cleared to give the player a bit of feedback and to tell them what to do next.

There are three different circumstances for which we want to display a message:

- Game over because the plane exploded.

- Game over because all four levels have been cleared.

- A level has been cleared.

In each case, we will also tell the user that they can hit the return key to continue.

We can work out if the game is over because the variable plane_ exploded will be True.

We can work out if the level has been cleared because the variable level_cleared will be True.

We can use the following line of code (Figure 5-7) to test if the game is over or the level has been cleared.

```
if plane_exploded is True or level_cleared is True:
```

Figure 5-7. *Tests if game is over or level is cleared*

We can now use more specific if statements to decide which message should be displayed.

To test if it is game over, use the code in Figure 5-8.

```
if plane_exploded is True:
```

Figure 5-8. *Tests if game is over*

To test if the player has cleared all four levels, use the code in Figure 5-9.

```
elif level == TOTAL_LEVELS:
```

Figure 5-9. *Tests if player has cleared all levels*

To test if one of the levels 1–3 has been cleared, we can use an `else` statement. An else statement is used with `if` and `elif` statements to say 'Well, if it was none of the above, then do this.'

The logic to an else statement looks like this:

if it is game over

run this code

else if the player has cleared all levels

run this code

else

run this code

So the code following the else statement will run if it is not game over and the player has not cleared all levels. Therefore, it can only be that the player has completed one of the levels 1–3.

Displaying a message on screen in Pygame is relatively straightforward. Getting the message to appear neatly is a bit trickier. We want our messages to be displayed

- As white text

- On a blue rectangle

- Centered vertically

- Centered horizontally

Add code block 23 (Figure 5-10) at line 241 which will work out the correct text message to be displayed.

```
level_text = 'Level: ' + str(level)
text = font.render(level_text, True, PURPLE)
text_rect = text.get_rect()
game_screen.blit(text, {(SCREEN_WIDTH - text_rect.width) / 2, SCOREBOARD_MARGIN})

# End of game / level message
if plane_exploded is True or level_cleared is True:

    if plane_exploded is True:
        text_line_1 = font.render('GAME OVER', True, WHITE)
        text_rect_1 = text_line_1.get_rect()

        text_line_2 = font.render('RETURN for new game', True, WHITE)
        text_rect_2 = text_line_2.get_rect()

        if plane_explode_sound_played is False:
            explosion_sound.play()
            plane_explode_sound_played = True

    elif level == TOTAL_LEVELS:
        text_line_1 = font.render('GAME OVER - ALL LEVELS CLEARED', True, WHITE)
        text_rect_1 = text_line_1.get_rect()

        text_line_2 = font.render('RETURN for new game', True, WHITE)
        text_rect_2 = text_line_2.get_rect()

    else:
        text_line_1 = font.render('LEVEL ' + str(level) + ' CLEARED', True, WHITE)
        text_rect_1 = text_line_1.get_rect()

        text_line_2 = font.render('RETURN for new level', True, WHITE)
        text_rect_2 = text_line_2.get_rect()

pygame.display.update()
clock.tick(30)
```

Figure 5-10.   *Forest Bomber code listing 23*

Now insert code block 24 (Figure 5-11) at line 269. Take particular care when entering lines 274 and 276. They are actually both single lines of code, but they are too long to fit a single line, and so they wrap over two separate lines. To enter these lines, type the code up to and including the command and then hit return. The cursor will line up in the correct place.

We won't be examining this code block too closely, but in summary it does all of the math needed to draw the blue box and center the text neatly on top of it.

```
        else:
            text_line_1 = font.render('LEVEL ' + str(level) + ' CLEARED', True, WHITE)
            text_rect_1 = text_line_1.get_rect()

            text_line_2 = font.render('RETURN for new level', True, WHITE)
            text_rect_2 = text_line_2.get_rect()

        # Display message box to sit text over
        msg_bk_rect = ((SCREEN_WIDTH - BOX_WIDTH) / 2, (SCREEN_HEIGHT - BOX_HEIGHT) / 2, BOX_WIDTH, BOX_HEIGHT)
        pygame.draw.rect(game_screen, DARK_BLUE, msg_bk_rect)

        # Display 2 lines of text, centred
        game_screen.blit(text_line_1, ((SCREEN_WIDTH - text_rect_1.width) / 2,
                                        (SCREEN_HEIGHT - text_rect_1.height) / 2 - LINE_HEIGHT))
        game_screen.blit(text_line_2, ((SCREEN_WIDTH - text_rect_2.width) / 2,
                                        (SCREEN_HEIGHT - text_rect_2.height) / 2 + LINE_HEIGHT))

    pygame.display.update()
    clock.tick(30)
```

Figure 5-11. *Forest Bomber code listing 24*

Run the game. A message should be displayed when it is game over or when a level is cleared.

Key learning   The Python `else` statement is used with `if` and `elif` and will be executed if none of the previous statements evaluate to True.

Congratulations – you have completed your first full Python/Pygame game.

Now you are probably thinking something along the lines of 'OK...but I only understood a little of how Forest Bomber works, and there's certainly no way I could write my own game!'

This is to be expected. We have covered a lot of complex programming concepts writing Forest Bomber. Instead, here are the five key learning elements that you should hopefully be able to take away from coding Forest Bomber:

Forest Bomber five key learning elements:

1. A variable is used to store a value. Each variable has its own unique name.

2. To add a value onto a variable, we use +=.

3. To test if two values are equal, we use ==.

4. The blit keyword is used to draw graphics onto the screen at given coordinates.

5. The if keyword is used to make a decision, and it is commonly used with elif and else.

## CHAPTER 6

Snapper part 1: In the woods

Charlotte was awake even before her alarm clock told her it was time to get up. She pulled back the curtains just far enough to see that the sun was already beating down. It was Saturday morning, and today was going to be a perfect day for it.

Charlotte sprang out of bed, threw on her clothes, and began packing the equipment that she would need for the day ahead: a rucksack, a cheese sandwich, plenty of water, and most importantly her prized possession – the Canon SLR camera that her grandfather had given her when she was just 8 years old.

Getting started

Snapper is a simple first-person shooting game where the aim is to target forest animals. However, as we don't actually want to kill any of our furry friends, we will be using a camera instead of a gun.

The animals will appear in random locations around the forest backdrop. To make the game more challenging, an animal will only appear for a brief period of time before going into hiding again.

© Mark Cunningham 2020
M. Cunningham, *Game Programming with Code Angel*,
https://doi.org/10.1007/978-1-4842-5305-2_6

Now that we have the overall game idea, we need to break it down into smaller steps:

1. Set up the game environment.

2. Initialize variables.

3. Display the background.

4. Draw and move the camera.

5. Show an animal.

6. Hide an animal.

7. Take a photograph.

8. Game over.

9. Scoreboard.

You will spot that some of these steps are very similar to the Forest Bomber design, but steps 4–7 are different.

Let's check out how the finished game will look (Figure 6-1).

The player will move the camera using the mouse, and the animals (in this example a rabbit) will appear at a random location on screen.

The player must try and photograph each animal before it hides again. Clicking the mouse button will take a photograph.

Figure 6-1. *Snapper design*

Step 1: Set up the game environment

The setup for Snapper is very similar to that of Forest Bomber, and indeed all of the games covered in this book. Enter code listing 1 (Figure 6-2).

```
 1    #!/usr/bin/python
 2    # Snapper
 3    # Code Angel
 4
 5    import sys
 6    import os
 7    import pygame
 8    from pygame.locals import *
 9    import random
10
11    # Define the colours
12    DARK_GREEN = (0, 98, 7)
13    DARK_GREY = (70, 70, 70)
14    WHITE = (255, 255, 255)
15
16    # Define constants
17    SCREEN_WIDTH = 640
18    SCREEN_HEIGHT = 480
19    SCOREBOARD_HEIGHT = 24
20    SCOREBOARD_MARGIN = 4
21
22    # Camera viewfinder constants
23    CAM_LEFT_BORDER = 9
24    VIEWFINDER_WIDTH = 44
25    CAM_TOP_BORDER = 21
26    VIEWFINDER_HEIGHT = 30
27
28    GAME_LIVES = 3
29
```

Figure 6-2. *Snapper code listing 1*

As with Forest Bomber, we import some Python and Pygame libraries and some colors; and then from line 17 onward, we set up some of the constant values that we will be using in the program. Enter code listing 2 (Figure 6-3).

```
30    # Setup
31    os.environ['SDL_VIDEO_CENTERED'] = '1'
32    pygame.mixer.pre_init(44100, -16, 2, 512)
33    pygame.mixer.init()
34    pygame.init()
35    game_screen = pygame.display.set_mode((SCREEN_WIDTH, SCREEN_HEIGHT))
36    pygame.display.set_caption('Snapper')
37    clock = pygame.time.Clock()
38    font = pygame.font.SysFont('Arial Narrow Bold', 24)
39
40
41    # Load images
42    background_image = pygame.image.load('background.png').convert()
43    foreground_image = pygame.image.load('foreground.png').convert_alpha()
44    camera_image = pygame.image.load('camera.png').convert_alpha()
45    camera_flash_image = pygame.image.load('camera_flash.png').convert_alpha()
46    lives_image = pygame.image.load('camera_lives.png').convert_alpha()
47    snap_image = pygame.image.load('snap.png').convert_alpha()
48    miss_image = pygame.image.load('miss.png').convert_alpha()
49    rabbit_image = pygame.image.load('rabbit.png').convert_alpha()
50    owl_image = pygame.image.load('owl.png').convert_alpha()
51    deer_image = pygame.image.load('deer.png').convert_alpha()
52    squirrel_image = pygame.image.load('squirrel.png').convert_alpha()
53
54    # Load sounds
55    camera_sound = pygame.mixer.Sound('click.ogg')
56    miss_sound = pygame.mixer.Sound('miss.ogg')
57
58
```

Figure 6-3. *Snapper code listing 2*

We also need to

- Set up the game window (lines 31–38).

- Load the Snapper graphics (lines 42–53).

- Load the Snapper audio files (lines 55 and 56).

Step 2: Initialize variables

Remember a variable is like a box. It stores a piece of information or data to be used in the program. At the beginning of the program, we give each variable an initial value, and we call this process initialization. Figure 6-4 shows the first set of variables used in Snapper.

```
59    def main():
60
61        # initialize variables
62        mouse_button_pressed = False
63
64        snap_visible = False
65        miss_visible = False
66
67        pygame.mouse.set_visible(False)
68
69        animal_rect = pygame.Rect(0, 0, 0, 0)
70
```

Figure 6-4. *Snapper code listing 3*

Notice def main(): at line 59. This indicates that everything that follows is the main part of the program. Pay particular attention to the indentation from line 61 onward, and remember that each level of indentation should be exactly four spaces (or one tab) from the left-hand side.

Boolean variables

Let's take a closer look at the first three variables shown in the code listing: mouse_button_pressed, snap_visible, and miss_visible. Each of these variables will store one of two possible values:

True or False

As we learned in Chapter 3, variables that store only `True` or `False` are known as Boolean variables.

- `mouse_button_pressed` is set to `False` to indicate that the mouse button has not been pressed. Later in the program, we will set the value of `mouse_button_pressed` to `True` when the player clicks the mouse button.

- `snap_visible` and `miss_visible` are also set to `False`. When the player attempts to take a photograph, we will display a tick or a cross over the camera image to show whether or not they snapped the animal, as shown in Figure 6-5.

Figure 6-5. *Showing what happens when snap_visible (left) and miss_visible (right) are True*

Finally, line 67 hides the mouse pointer. This is important because we don't want the pointer to appear when we move the mouse around the game window. We want to show the camera image in its place.

Key learning   A *Boolean variable* can store one of two values: `True` or `False`.

Dictionaries

There are still some more variables that need to be initialized at the start of the game. One of these is a special type of variable used in Python called a *dictionary*. A dictionary is useful when storing multiple data items about an object. Each value in a dictionary can be identified by its unique key.

The `animals` dictionary is shown in Figure 6-6. You might want to take a deep breath before keying it into your program!

```
71      # Dictionary to store the animals
72      animals = {
73          'animal_1': {'type': 'rabbit', 'x_loc': 290, 'y_loc': 130, 'time': 60, 'points': 10},
74          'animal_2': {'type': 'rabbit', 'x_loc': 332, 'y_loc': 318, 'time': 60, 'points': 10},
75          'animal_3': {'type': 'rabbit', 'x_loc': 96, 'y_loc': 304, 'time': 60, 'points': 10},
76          'animal_4': {'type': 'rabbit', 'x_loc': 358, 'y_loc': 159, 'time': 60, 'points': 10},
77          'animal_5': {'type': 'rabbit', 'x_loc': 464, 'y_loc': 155, 'time': 60, 'points': 10},
78          'animal_6': {'type': 'rabbit', 'x_loc': 202, 'y_loc': 297, 'time': 60, 'points': 10},
79          'animal_7': {'type': 'rabbit', 'x_loc': 265, 'y_loc': 318, 'time': 60, 'points': 10},
80          'animal_8': {'type': 'rabbit', 'x_loc': 363, 'y_loc': 344, 'time': 60, 'points': 10},
81          'animal_9': {'type': 'owl', 'x_loc': 387, 'y_loc': 46, 'time': 75, 'points': 5},
82          'animal_10': {'type': 'owl', 'x_loc': 295, 'y_loc': 47, 'time': 75, 'points': 5},
83          'animal_11': {'type': 'owl', 'x_loc': 474, 'y_loc': 235, 'time': 75, 'points': 5},
84          'animal_12': {'type': 'owl', 'x_loc': 574, 'y_loc': 132, 'time': 75, 'points': 5},
85          'animal_13': {'type': 'owl', 'x_loc': 23, 'y_loc': 126, 'time': 75, 'points': 5},
86          'animal_14': {'type': 'squirrel', 'x_loc': 17, 'y_loc': 113, 'time': 40, 'points': 20},
87          'animal_15': {'type': 'squirrel', 'x_loc': 567, 'y_loc': 124, 'time': 40, 'points': 20},
88          'animal_16': {'type': 'squirrel', 'x_loc': 448, 'y_loc': 278, 'time': 40, 'points': 20},
89          'animal_17': {'type': 'squirrel', 'x_loc': 452, 'y_loc': 359, 'time': 40, 'points': 20},
90          'animal_18': {'type': 'squirrel', 'x_loc': 304, 'y_loc': 301, 'time': 40, 'points': 20},
91          'animal_19': {'type': 'squirrel', 'x_loc': 62, 'y_loc': 279, 'time': 40, 'points': 20},
92          'animal_20': {'type': 'deer', 'x_loc': 106, 'y_loc': 87, 'time': 90, 'points': 1},
93          'animal_21': {'type': 'deer', 'x_loc': 268, 'y_loc': 84, 'time': 90, 'points': 1},
94          'animal_22': {'type': 'deer', 'x_loc': 302, 'y_loc': 90, 'time': 90, 'points': 1},
95          'animal_23': {'type': 'deer', 'x_loc': 392, 'y_loc': 127, 'time': 90, 'points': 1}
96      }
97
```

Figure 6-6. *Snapper code listing 4*

Care should be taken when typing the `animals` dictionary into the program. Every bracket, every comma, and every quote mark must be included; or the program will not work. Pay attention to the brackets also – they are curly brackets { } as opposed to curved brackets ( ).

By now you will be wondering what is the point of the `animals` dictionary. It stores data about all of the animals in the Snapper game. This will make more sense if we zoom in on one of the lines. Let's say line 73.

Line 73 is a dictionary element. It stores information about `animal_1`. `animal_1` is known as the *key* of this dictionary element, and everything after it is the *value*. The value stored is itself a dictionary which stores the data about `animal_1`, specifically

- `type`: The type of animal (can be rabbit, owl, squirrel, or deer)

- `x_loc`: The x coordinate of the location where the animal will appear on screen

- y_loc: The y coordinate of the location where the animal will appear on screen

- time: The length of time before the animal hides again

- points: The score multiplier that will be awarded if the animal is successfully photographed

All 23 animals in the game are stored in the animals dictionary.

Key learning   A *dictionary* is used to store data items in key/value pairs.

We just have a few more variables to initialize before we can crack on with the main game code. These are shown in Figure 6-7.

```
98    no_animal_timer = 0
99
100   animal_visible = True
101
102   score = 0
103   lives = GAME_LIVES
104   hi_score = 0
105
```

Figure 6-7. *Snapper code listing 5*

These variables can be described as follows:

- no_animal_timer: Used to measure the time between one animal hiding and another animal appearing

- animal_visible: Boolean value used to indicate whether an animal is presently being shown on screen

- score: The current game score

- lives: The number of lives the player has remaining

- hi_score: The current game high score

Step 3: Display the background

With all variables now initialized, our next step is to display the game background. Enter the remaining code shown in Figure 6-8.

```
106    # Main game loop
107    while True:
108
109        # Check for mouse and key presses
110        for event in pygame.event.get():
111
112            # User quits
113            if event.type == QUIT:
114                pygame.quit()
115                sys.exit()
116
117        # Draw background
118        game_screen.blit(background_image, [0, 0])
119
120        # Draw the foreground overlay image
121        game_screen.blit(foreground_image, [0, 0])
122
123        pygame.display.update()
124        clock.tick(60)
125
126
127    if __name__ == '__main__':
128        main()
```

Figure 6-8. *Snapper code listing 6*

When we coded Forest Bomber, we used a while True loop, and we can see it again here at line 107. But what does it do? It is a loop which will go round and round forever. A while True loop is useful in game programming because we want our game code to loop continually – or at least until the player quits the game.

- Lines 113–115 deal with the user quitting the game by clicking the close button. When this happens, a QUIT event will be triggered, and this code will be run, exiting the Snapper program.

- Line 118 uses blit to draw the background onto the screen at coordinates (0,0). We saw this in Forest Bomber.

- Line 121 seems to be very similar to line 118, but it uses foreground_image as opposed to background_image. Why is this? foreground_image is actually an overlay image. It has cutouts, and this is where the animals will appear. foreground_image sits directly on top of background_image. You can get a better idea of how this will work if you open the file foreground.png which is one of the Snapper image files.

- Finally, lines 127 and 128 will start the main program – that is everything that comes after the line def main():.

Key learning   A while True *loop* will repeat forever.

Once again, it has taken us some time to write a lot of code, with only a single static screen to show for our efforts. In the following chapters, we will develop the actual Snapper game functionality...

CHAPTER 7

Snapper part 2: Say cheese

Charlotte waved goodbye to her mother as she started off on the trail heading north toward the forest. The sun's rays warmed her back as she walked, with only the occasional birdsong cutting through the tranquility of the day.

After what seemed like no time at all, Charlotte found herself walking between the trees, their leaves and branches forming a shaded canopy above her head. She had arrived at a place that she knew well and which would give her an unobscured view of a clearing directly ahead.

Charlotte unpacked her Canon SLR and waited patiently.

In the last chapter, we set up the game environment and initialized the variables (including the `animals` dictionary variable which stores data about each of Snapper's animals). We also displayed the screen background.

Our next steps are the following:

4. Draw and move the camera.

5. Show an animal.

6. Hide an animal.

© Mark Cunningham 2020
M. Cunningham, *Game Programming with Code Angel*,
https://doi.org/10.1007/978-1-4842-5305-2_7

Step 4: Draw and move the camera

The mouse pointer

The camera's movement is going to be controlled by the mouse. We can do this quite easily. Insert the code shown in Figure 7-1 at line 117.

```
106     # Main game loop
107     while True:
108
109         # Check for mouse and key presses
110         for event in pygame.event.get():
111
112             # User quits
113             if event.type == QUIT:
114                 pygame.quit()
115                 sys.exit()
116
117         # Set the camera centre to the location of the mouse pointer
118         mouse_pos = pygame.mouse.get_pos()
119
120         camera_rect = camera_image.get_rect()
121         camera_rect.centerx = mouse_pos[0]
122         camera_rect.centery = mouse_pos[1]
123
124         # Draw background
125         game_screen.blit(background_image, [0, 0])
```

Figure 7-1. *Snapper code listing 7*

Line 118 gets the current mouse location using the Pygame mouse.get_pos() function. We store the mouse position in the variable mouse_pos.

The mouse position is stored as two values, one for the x coordinate of the mouse and the other for the y coordinate. To access the x coordinate, we use mouse_pos[0], and to access the y coordinate, we use mouse_pos[1].

We set the center of the camera to the x and y coordinates of the mouse in lines 121 and 122.

Next, we need to actually draw (blit) the camera onto the game background. Enter code listing 8 (Figure 7-2) at line 130 of the program.

```
187    # Draw the foreground overlay image
188    game_screen.blit(foreground_image, [0, 0])
189
190    # Draw Camera
191    if snap_visible is True or miss_visible is True:
192        game_screen.blit(camera_flash_image, camera_rect)
193    else:
194        game_screen.blit(camera_image, camera_rect)
195
196    pygame.display.update()
197    clock.tick(60)
```

Figure 7-2. *Snapper code listing 8*

Lines 131–134 draw either the normal camera image or the flash camera image. The if statement at line 131 works out whether snap_visible or miss_visible is True. We will make use of these variables later in the code, but for now we can see from looking back at lines 64 and 65, they are both initialized to False and so the camera_image will be displayed by line 134.

Run the program and move the mouse – the camera should move around the screen. That's pretty neat, but notice that the camera disappears off the edge of the screen. We don't want that to happen, so let's fix it. Add the code from Figure 7-3 at line 124.

```
117    # Set the camera centre to the location of the mouse pointer
118    mouse_pos = pygame.mouse.get_pos()
119
120    camera_rect = camera_image.get_rect()
121    camera_rect.centerx = mouse_pos[0]
122    camera_rect.centery = mouse_pos[1]
123
124    camera_width = camera_image.get_width()
125    camera_height = camera_image.get_height()
126
127    # Prevent the camera going off the screen
128    if camera_rect.centerx < camera_width / 2:
129        camera_rect.centerx = camera_width / 2
130    if camera_rect.centerx > SCREEN_WIDTH - camera_width / 2:
131        camera_rect.centerx = SCREEN_WIDTH - camera_width / 2
132
133    if camera_rect.centery < camera_height / 2:
134        camera_rect.centery = camera_height / 2
135    if camera_rect.centery > SCREEN_HEIGHT - camera_height / 2 - SCOREBOARD_HEIGHT:
136        camera_rect.centery = SCREEN_HEIGHT - camera_height / 2 - SCOREBOARD_HEIGHT
137
138    # Draw background
139    game_screen.blit(background_image, [0, 0])
```

Figure 7-3. *Snapper code listing 9*

What's going on here?

- Lines 124 and 125 get the camera width and height and store each in a variable.

- Lines 128 and 129 prevent the camera from going off the left edge of the screen, while lines 130 and 131 prevent it from going off the right edge of the screen.

- Lines 133 and 134 prevent the camera from moving off the top of the screen, while lines 135 and 136 stop it from going below the scoreboard which will appear at the bottom of the screen.

Key learning `pygame.mouse.get_pos()` can be used to get the coordinates of the mouse pointer.

Step 5: Show an animal

Using the dictionary

Remember that the data for all 23 animals is held in a fairly large dictionary called `animals`.

Our next challenge is to display one of the 23 animals on screen – but which one should we show? We want our program to choose one of the animals at random. Making random choices is one of the core fundamentals of game programming. After all, who wants to play a game that does exactly the same thing every time?

```
71    # Dictionary to store the animals
72    animals = {
73        'animal_1': {'type': 'rabbit', 'x_loc': 298, 'y_loc': 120, 'time': 40, 'points': 10},
74        'animal_2': {'type': 'rabbit', 'x_loc': 392, 'y_loc': 318, 'time': 60, 'points': 10},
75        'animal_3': {'type': 'rabbit', 'x_loc': 96, 'y_loc': 304, 'time': 60, 'points': 10},
76        'animal_4': {'type': 'rabbit', 'x_loc': 358, 'y_loc': 159, 'time': 40, 'points': 10},
77        'animal_5': {'type': 'rabbit', 'x_loc': 466, 'y_loc': 155, 'time': 60, 'points': 10},
78        'animal_6': {'type': 'rabbit', 'x_loc': 202, 'y_loc': 297, 'time': 60, 'points': 10},
79        'animal_7': {'type': 'rabbit', 'x_loc': 265, 'y_loc': 318, 'time': 60, 'points': 10},
80        'animal_8': {'type': 'rabbit', 'x_loc': 367, 'y_loc': 344, 'time': 60, 'points': 10},
81        'animal_9': {'type': 'owl', 'x_loc': 387, 'y_loc': 46, 'time': 75, 'points': 5},
82        'animal_10': {'type': 'owl', 'x_loc': 295, 'y_loc': 47, 'time': 75, 'points': 5},
83        'animal_11': {'type': 'owl', 'x_loc': 474, 'y_loc': 235, 'time': 75, 'points': 5},
84        'animal_12': {'type': 'owl', 'x_loc': 574, 'y_loc': 132, 'time': 75, 'points': 5},
85        'animal_13': {'type': 'owl', 'x_loc': 23, 'y_loc': 128, 'time': 75, 'points': 5},
86        'animal_14': {'type': 'squirrel', 'x_loc': 17, 'y_loc': 113, 'time': 40, 'points': 20},
87        'animal_15': {'type': 'squirrel', 'x_loc': 567, 'y_loc': 124, 'time': 40, 'points': 20},
88        'animal_16': {'type': 'squirrel', 'x_loc': 445, 'y_loc': 278, 'time': 40, 'points': 20},
89        'animal_17': {'type': 'squirrel', 'x_loc': 452, 'y_loc': 359, 'time': 40, 'points': 20},
90        'animal_18': {'type': 'squirrel', 'x_loc': 304, 'y_loc': 301, 'time': 40, 'points': 20},
91        'animal_19': {'type': 'squirrel', 'x_loc': 62, 'y_loc': 278, 'time': 40, 'points': 20},
92        'animal_20': {'type': 'deer', 'x_loc': 108, 'y_loc': 87, 'time': 90, 'points': 1},
93        'animal_21': {'type': 'deer', 'x_loc': 268, 'y_loc': 84, 'time': 90, 'points': 1},
94        'animal_22': {'type': 'deer', 'x_loc': 302, 'y_loc': 90, 'time': 90, 'points': 1},
95        'animal_23': {'type': 'deer', 'x_loc': 392, 'y_loc': 127, 'time': 90, 'points': 1}
96    }

98    random_animal = random.choice(list(animals.keys()))
99    animal = animals.get(random_animal)
```

***Figure 7-4.** Snapper code listing 10*

Add the two new lines of code shown in Figure 7-4 at lines 98 and 99.

Line 98 makes use of Python's `random.choice` function which picks an item from a list at random. Our code picks a random animal from the `animals` dictionary.

In fact, `random.choice` actually gets one of the random animal keys, for example, `animal_14` or `animal_21`. What we really want is the animals dictionary represented by that key. Line 99 initializes the `animal` variable with the dictionary represented by the random key.

For example, let's say that line 98 randomly selected the key `animal_7`. Line 99 stores the dictionary representing `animal_7` in the `animal` variable, so `animal` would look like this:

```
{'type': 'rabbit', 'x_loc': 265, 'y_loc': 318, 'time': 60,
'points': 10}
```

Now that we have a random animals dictionary, let's use it to display the animal on screen. Remember that `'type'` stores the type of animal to be displayed, while `'x_loc'` and `'y_loc'` are the animal's coordinates.

```
140        # Draw background
141        game_screen.blit(background_image, [0, 0])
142
143        # If there is an animal visible, draw animal
144        if animal_visible is True:
145            animal_x = int(animal.get('x_loc'))
146            animal_y = int(animal.get('y_loc'))
147
148            # Blit the correct animal onto the screen on top of background but below foreground
149            if animal.get('type') == 'rabbit':
150                game_screen.blit(rabbit_image, [animal_x, animal_y])
151            elif animal.get('type') == 'owl':
152                game_screen.blit(owl_image, [animal_x, animal_y])
153            elif animal.get('type') == 'deer':
154                game_screen.blit(deer_image, [animal_x, animal_y])
155            else:
156                game_screen.blit(squirrel_image, [animal_x, animal_y])
157
158        # Draw the foreground overlay image
159        game_screen.blit(foreground_image, [0, 0])
```

Figure 7-5. *Snapper code listing 11*

Add the block of code shown in Figure 7-5 at line 143 of the program. Notice that we are drawing the animal after the background but before the foreground overlay. With blit, each image is drawn on top of any previously drawn images. In Snapper we draw the screen elements in the following order:

- The background

- The animal

- The foreground overlay

Using the foreground overlay in this way, we can partially hide our animals behind trees, bushes, or even hills.

Examining code listing 11 we can see that:

- Line 143 uses a Boolean variable called animal_visible which was initialized to True at the start of the program. Later in the program we will set it to False to hide the animal, but for now animal_visible is True. When set to True, the code between lines 145 and 156 will run, and the correct animal image will be displayed.

- Lines 145 and 146 get the values of the animal's x and y coordinates from the `animals` dictionary. To get a dictionary item from a dictionary, we use the dictionary's key. So

```
animal.get('x_loc'))
```

  gets the `x_loc` from the `animals` dictionary.

- Lines 149–156 work out the type of animal and then display its image at coordinates [`animal_x,animal_y`]. Again, notice the use of the dictionary key to get the animal type:

```
animal.get('type')
```

Now when you run the program, a random animal should be displayed. Quit the game, and then run it again. A different animal should be displayed in a new location.

Key learning   Use `random.choice` to randomly select an item from a list.

To get a value from a dictionary, use `dictionary_name.get('key_name')`.

Step 6: Hide an animal

Now that we have a random animal on screen, we want it to remain visible for a short time and then disappear. If the animal didn't disappear it would make it too easy to take a photograph and the game would become boring.

Setting a timer

If we look again at the animals dictionary, we will see that each animal has a key 'time'. The value represented by the key 'time' is the length of time that the animal will remain on screen.

Before we can hide an animal, we need to first get the time value by using the 'time' key.

Add line 100 as shown in Figure 7-6.

```
98    random_animal = random.choice(list(animals.keys()))
99    animal = animals.get(random_animal)
100   animal_timer = animal.get('time')
101   no_animal_timer = 0
```

Figure 7-6. *Snapper code listing 12*

Line 100 assigns the dictionary value of the animal 'time' to the animal_timer.

Next we have to count down the timer and hide the animal when it reaches 0. Add code listing 13 as shown in Figure 7-7.

```
136   if camera_rect.centery < camera_height / 2:
137       camera_rect.centery = camera_height / 2
138   if camera_rect.centery > SCREEN_HEIGHT - camera_height / 2 - SCOREBOARD_HEIGHT:
139       camera_rect.centery = SCREEN_HEIGHT - camera_height / 2 - SCOREBOARD_HEIGHT
140
141   # If there is an animal visible, decrease the animal_timer and work out the animal rect
142   if animal_visible is True:
143       animal_timer -= 1
144
145       # If the animal timer reaches zero, hide the animal and pause
146       if animal_timer == 0:
147           no_animal_timer = random.randint(30, 120)
148           animal_visible = False
149
150       animal_x = animal.get('x_loc')
151       animal_y = animal.get('y_loc')
152
153       if animal.get('type') == 'rabbit':
154           animal_rect = pygame.Rect(animal_x, animal_y, rabbit_image.get_width(), rabbit_image.get_height())
155       elif animal.get('type') == 'owl':
156           animal_rect = pygame.Rect(animal_x, animal_y, owl_image.get_width(), owl_image.get_height())
157       elif animal.get('type') == 'deer':
158           animal_rect = pygame.Rect(animal_x, animal_y, deer_image.get_width(), deer_image.get_height())
159       else:
160           animal_rect = pygame.Rect(animal_x, animal_y, squirrel_image.get_width(), squirrel_image.get_height())
161
162   # Draw background
163   game_screen.blit(background_image, [0, 0])
```

Figure 7-7. *Snapper code listing 13*

Lines 142–148 handle our animal timer, but how do they work?

- Line 142 checks the animal_visible Boolean variable, and if it is True (the animal is currently on screen) we subtract 1 from the value of animal_timer at line 143. In Python, we subtract a value from a variable using -= (also note that we can add a value onto a variable using +=).

  Because the entire game code runs in a while True loop, the program will keep looping, subtracting 1 from animal_timer each time through the loop until the timer hits zero.

- Line 146 checks to see if animal_timer has reached 0. We have already learned that we use == in Python to check if two values are equal.

- If the animal_timer equals zero, then line 147 initializes a new variable called no_animal_timer. no_ animal_timer is used in a similar way to animal_timer, but it counts down the time until the next animal is displayed.

  We set no_animal_timer to a random value so that the length of time between one animal hiding and the next animal appearing is always different. Python's random.randint() function generates a random integer. In this case, we stipulate that the random number should be between 30 and 120.

- Finally at line 148, we set the animal_visible Boolean to False. Recall that we only display an animal if animal_visible is True. By setting the value of this variable to False, no animal will be displayed.

You may be wondering what these timer numbers actually equate to in real time. Look to the very bottom of the Snapper code, and you will see the line

```
clock.tick(60)
```

In simple terms, it means that the while True loop will execute 60 times every second. So if we look back at our dictionary, we see that the time value for animal_1 (a rabbit) is 60. That means it will be displayed on screen for exactly one second. By comparison, animal_23 (a deer) has the time value set to 90, so this animal will stay on screen for 1.5 seconds.

(Cheat hint: If you want to make the game easier, increase these time values.)

Rectangles

The code in Figure 7-7 has some additional lines which we have not explained yet.

Lines 150–160 are used to work out the size and location of the animal image currently on screen. Each image is actually a rectangle. We won't go into this code in much detail at the moment other than to say we use it to work out if the camera is on top of the animal when the player takes a photograph.

Key learning   We can use -= to subtract a value from a variable, for example, animal_timer -= 1 will subtract 1 from the variable animal_timer.

Use random.randint() to generate a random number, for example, random.randint(1, 10) will generate a random number between 1 and 10.

Show another animal

Next, we need to count down the no_animal_timer and then display another random animal on screen.

```
# if the animal timer reaches zero, hide the animal and pause
if animal_timer == 0:
    no_animal_timer = random.randint(30, 120)
    animal_visible = False

animal_x = animal.get('x_loc')
animal_y = animal.get('y_loc')

if animal.get('type') == 'rabbit':
    animal_rect = pygame.Rect(animal_x, animal_y, rabbit_image.get_width(), rabbit_image.get_height())
elif animal.get('type') == 'owl':
    animal_rect = pygame.Rect(animal_x, animal_y, owl_image.get_width(), owl_image.get_height())
elif animal.get('type') == 'deer':
    animal_rect = pygame.Rect(animal_x, animal_y, deer_image.get_width(), deer_image.get_height())
else:
    animal_rect = pygame.Rect(animal_x, animal_y, squirrel_image.get_width(), squirrel_image.get_height())

# Countdown the no animal timer, and when it hits zero get a new animal
if animal_visible is False:
    no_animal_timer -= 1

    if no_animal_timer == 0:
        if lives > 0:
            random_animal = random.choice(list(animals.keys()))
            animal = animals.get(random_animal)
            animal_timer = animal.get('time')
            animal_visible = True

        snap_visible = False
        miss_visible = False

# Draw background
game_screen.blit(background_image, [0, 0])
```

Figure 7-8. *Snapper code listing 14*

Enter the code shown in Figure 7-8 at line 162. Let's take a look at it:

- Line 163 checks to see if the animal_visible is False; in other words, there is no animal currently being shown.

- If that's the case, we subtract 1 from the no_animal_timer at line 164.

- Line 166 checks to see if the no_animal_timer has reached 0.

- Line 167 then checks to see if we have any lives left.

81

- If the timer has reached 0, and we still have lives left, we need to generate a new random animal. For now, we will use exactly the same code as we did when generating a random animal earlier in the program at lines 168 and 169.

- Line 170 sets up the new `animal_timer` (we have seen this before at the start of the program).

- At line 171, we set the `animal_visible` variable to `True` so that the animal will be shown.

- Lastly, we set the values of the two Booleans `snap_visible` and `miss_visible` to `False`. We will see shortly how we make use of them.

Building a function

Notice how we generated a random animal at two different places in the program, once at the start of the code and then again when we wanted to get a new animal to show. Copying code in this way is not considered good practice. What happens, for example, if we change the code that generates a random animal? We would have to remember to change the code in both places.

Instead, it is better practice to build a single block of code to do this. In programming, it is common to break a program down into smaller blocks of code that carry out a specific task. In Python, these code blocks are called *functions*.

A function is a block of code that carries out a specific job. It may optionally `return` a value back into the main program when it has finished.

We will create a function to generate a random animal, and we will call our function `get_random_animal`. As with naming variables, we can call a function anything we wish, but it is good practice for the name of the function to describe what it does. So get_random_animal does exactly what it says on the tin!

```
194        # Draw the foreground overlay image
195        game_screen.blit(foreground_image, (0, 0))
196
197        # Draw Camera
198        if snap_visible is True or miss_visible is True:
199            game_screen.blit(camera_flash_image, camera_rect)
200        else:
201            game_screen.blit(camera_image, camera_rect)
202
203        pygame.display.update()
204        clock.tick(60)
205
206
207    # Get a random animal from the dictionary
208    def get_random_animal(animals):
209        random_animal = random.choice(list(animals.keys()))
210        return animals.get(random_animal)
211
212
213    if __name__ == '__main__':
214        main()
```

Figure 7-9. *Snapper code listing 15*

Enter the function code as shown in Figure 7-9 near the foot of the program. Notice the use of two blank lines above and below the function.

Next, we need to go back to our main program and change the code so that it makes use of this function instead.

Replace lines 98 and 99 of the program shown in Figure 7-10 with the single line of code shown in Figure 7-11.

```
98        random_animal = random.choice(list(animals.keys()))
99        animal = animals.get(random_animal)
```

Figure 7-10. *Code to be replaced*

```
98        animal = get_random_animal(animals)
99        animal_timer = animal.get('time')
100       no_animal_timer = 0
```

Figure 7-11. *Snapper code listing 16*

Similarly, replace lines 167 and 168 shown in Figure 7-12 with the single line of code shown in Figure 7-13.

```
167    random_animal = random.choice(list(animals.keys()))
168    animal = animals.get(random_animal)
```

Figure 7-12. *Code to be replaced*

```
100    if no_animal_timer == 0:
101        if lives > 0:
102            animal = get_random_animal(animals)
103            animal_timer = animal.get('time')
104            animal_visible = True
```

Figure 7-13. *Snapper code listing 17*

The code works like this:

1. The program reaches line 98:

    animal = get_random_animal(animals).

2. Python doesn't know what get_random_animals is,
    so it looks to see if there is a function by that name.
    Of course, there is:

    def get_random_animal(animals):

3. Did you notice in the main program the word
    animals is between the brackets? This is known as a
    parameter, and we are going to pass this parameter
    into the function. Remember that animals is our
    dictionary which stores data about all of the animals
    in Snapper.

4. Look again at the get_random_animal function. It
    also has the word animals between the brackets.
    The animals dictionary will be passed from the
    main program into the function where it will also be
    known as animals. We can now access the animals
    dictionary in our function.

5. The two lines of the function are almost exactly the same as the two lines of code that we replaced in the main program. However, there is one key difference. At the end of the function, it returns the random animal. But what does that mean? If we look back up to line 98, we see that

    ```
    animal = get_random_animal(animals).
    ```

    The function therefore returns the random animal, and it is assigned to the variable animal in the main program.

When our main program code runs a function, we say that it *calls* the function.

Don't worry if you find the concept of functions a bit tricky to understand – we will be revisiting functions again later in the book.

Key learning   Functions are blocks of code that carry out a specific task. Parameters can be passed into a function, and a result can be returned out of the function back to the main program.

We can see that Snapper is beginning to take shape. In the next chapter, we will see how we can tie all the parts of the game together by writing the code which will take a photograph.

CHAPTER 8

Snapper part 3: Snapped

Charlotte lay perfectly still, her breathing almost inaudible. All that she could hear was the sound of her own heart thumping in her chest. Her eyes scanned between the trees. Over there. Was that something moving, or was it her imagination? A cracking twig broke the silence.

Charlotte's gaze focused. There was something. A mere silhouette, she could see a head maybe, but what was it? Too big for a rabbit. She could almost make it out now, copper-brown fur the color of scorched earth, a lighter tail only just visible.

A deer stood less than 30 meters in front of Charlotte, staring right back at her.

With the most subtle of movements, she picked up her camera and zoomed in.

So far, our game has animals appearing and then hiding, and we can control the location of the camera by moving the mouse. In order for Snapper to become a game, we need to be able to take photographs.

© Mark Cunningham 2020
M. Cunningham, *Game Programming with Code Angel*,
https://doi.org/10.1007/978-1-4842-5305-2_8

The final stages of the game are

7.   Taking a photograph

8.   Game over

9.   Scoreboard

Step 7: Take a photograph

The player will take a photo by clicking the mouse button. Pygame has a
MOUSEBUTTONDOWN event which registers when the mouse button is pressed.

```
108     # Main game loop
109     while True:
110
111         # Check for mouse and key presses
112         for event in pygame.event.get():
113
114             # Mouse button clicked
115             mouse_button_pressed = False
116             if event.type == pygame.MOUSEBUTTONDOWN:
117                 mouse_button_pressed = True
118
119             # User quits
120             if event.type == QUIT:
121                 pygame.quit()
122                 sys.exit()
```

Figure 8-1. Snapper code listing 18

Add the code in Figure 8-1 at line 114. With this code, we check to see
if the mouse button is clicked and if so set the variable mouse_button_
pressed to True. Otherwise, it will remain False.

To find out what will be in the photo, we need to work out what can be
seen through the camera's viewfinder. The viewfinder is a rectangle, the
dimensions of which we can calculate.

```
if camera_rect.centery < camera_height / 2:
    camera_rect.centery = camera_height / 2
if camera_rect.centery > SCREEN_HEIGHT - camera_height / 2 - SCOREBOARD_HEIGHT:
    camera_rect.centery = SCREEN_HEIGHT - camera_height / 2 - SCOREBOARD_HEIGHT

# Calculate the camera's viewfinder rectangle
viewfinder_left = camera_rect.left + CAM_LEFT_BORDER
viewfinder_top = camera_rect.top + CAM_TOP_BORDER
viewfinder_rect = pygame.Rect(viewfinder_left, viewfinder_top, VIEWFINDER_WIDTH, VIEWFINDER_HEIGHT)

# If there is an animal visible, decrease the animal timer and work out the animal rect
if animal_visible is True:
    animal_timer -= 1
```

Figure 8-2. *Snapper code listing 19*

Add the code from Figure 8-2 at line 145 to calculate the viewfinder rectangle.

Rectangles collide

Next, we need to write some code to take a photograph when the mouse button is pressed. We will build this code block up in smaller parts.

```
# Countdown the no animal timer, and when it hits zero get a new animal
if animal_visible is False:
    no_animal_timer -= 1

    if no_animal_timer == 0:
        if lives > 0:
            animal = get_random_animal(animals)
            animal_timer = animal.get('time')
            animal_visible = True

        snap_visible = False
        miss_visible = False

# The player has clicked the mouse to take a photograph
if mouse_button_pressed is True:
    if snap_visible is False and miss_visible is false and lives > 0:

        # Check to see whether they got the animal in the viewfinder, and that the animal is visible
        if viewfinder_rect.colliderect(animal_rect):
            if animal_visible is True:
                score += animal_timer * animal.get('points')
                snap_visible = True
                camera_sound.play()

# Draw background
game_screen.blit(background_image, (0, 0))
```

Figure 8-3. *Snapper code listing 20*

Insert the code shown in Figure 8-3 at line 184. There are quite a lot of `if` statements here, so let's see what each one does:

- The `if` statement at line 178 is relatively straightforward – it is testing to see if a photo has been taken. A photo will have been taken if `mouse_button_pressed` has been set to `True`. Remember we set `mouse_button_pressed` to `True` when Pygame detects a `MOUSEBUTTONDOWN` event.

- The `if` statement at line 179 checks three variables. The first two, `snap_visible` and `miss_visible`, will be covered later. The third check is to find out whether `lives` > 0. When the game is over, `lives` will be 0, so here we are checking that the game is not over.

- The if statement on line 189 uses a really important Pygame function called `colliderect`. `colliderect` is important when writing games because it takes two rectangles and checks if they have collided with each other. We can use `colliderect` in games to test if a missile has hit a spaceship, if a racing car has driven over a patch of oil, or, in the case of Snapper, if the animal is in the camera viewfinder.

  `colliderect` takes the format `rectangle_1.collide_rect(rectangle_2)`.

  It will return `True` if the rectangles have collided and `False` if they have not collided.

  Figure 8-4 illustrates how `colliderect` works.

- The `if` statement on line 190 tests to see if the animal is visible. If the player takes a photo when there is no animal, then it will count as a failed photo.

Snapped it!

So the player has taken a photo if all of the following are true:

- The mouse button is pressed.

- It is not game over.

- The animal is in the camera's viewfinder.

- The animal is actually visible.

The code between lines 191 and 193 is run when these events happen:

- Line 191 calculates how much time was left on the timer, multiplies that by the points value for the animal, and adds the result onto the game score.

- Line 192 sets snap_visible to True. When snap_visible is True, a green tick will display in the camera viewfinder, and we can't take another photo.

- Line 193 plays an audio file – the camera shutter effect.

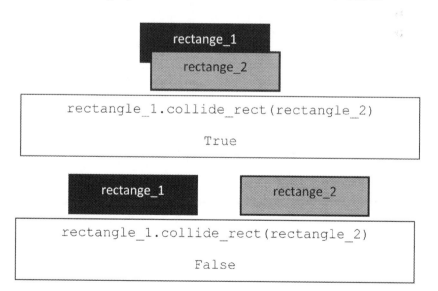

Figure 8-4. *Illustration of the Pygame colliderect() function*

Run the program and try to take a picture. If you are successful, you will hear the camera shutter sound effect being played, and the camera screen will go black. If you are unsuccessful, well, nothing happens, not yet anyway. Let's fix that.

Oops, missed!

Enter the code shown in Figure 8-5. Take particular care to ensure the indentation is exactly as shown in the code listing.

```
194       # The player has clicked the mouse to take a photograph
195       if mouse_button_pressed is True:
196           if snap_visible is False and miss_visible is False and lives > 0:
197
198               # Check to see whether they got the animal in the viewfinder, and that the animal is visible
199               if viewfinder_rect.colliderect(animal_rect):
190                   if animal_visible is True:
191                       score += animal_timer * animal.get('points')
192                       snap_visible = True
193                       camera_sound.play()
194
195                   else:
196                       miss_visible = True
197                       lives -= 1
198                       miss_sound.play()
199
200               else:
201                   miss_visible = True
202                   lives -= 1
203                   miss_sound.play()
204
205               # Hide the animal and pause
206               animal_visible = False
207               animal_timer = 0
208               no_animal_timer = 120
209
210       # Draw background
211       game_screen.blit(background_image, [0, 0])
```

Figure 8-5. *Snapper code listing 21*

The first else statement shown at line 195 goes with the statement

if animal_visible is True:

So the else statement will be reached if animal_visible is False. If the player tries to take a photograph when the animal is not visible (in other words, the animal disappeared before they could take the photo), then lines 196–198 will be run:

- Line 196 sets miss_visible to True. miss_visible is a Boolean variable very similar to snap_visible, but it will be used to show a red cross instead of a green tick.

- Line 197 subtracts one from the number of lives that the player has.

- Line 198 plays a buzzer sound effect to indicate that the photo was unsuccessful.

The second else statement at line 200 goes with the statement

if viewfinder_rect.colliderect(animal_rect):

This else statement will be reached if the viewfinder rectangle did not collide with the animal rectangle. In other words, the player missed the animal when they took their photograph. If this happens, lines 201–203 will be run, which as we can see do exactly the same thing as lines 196–198.

Whether the photo was successful or not, we run lines 206–208 to hide the animal, cancel the animal timer, and start a no animal timer.

Hit or miss?

Finally, we want to use the Boolean variables snap_visible and hit_visible in order to display a green tick or a red cross over the viewfinder to indicate whether or not the photograph was successful.

```
231     # Draw Camera
232     if snap_visible is True or miss_visible is True:
233         game_screen.blit(camera_flash_image, camera_rect)
234     else:
235         game_screen.blit(camera_image, camera_rect)
236
237     # Draw the snap or miss image
238     snap_or_miss_border = (VIEWFINDER_WIDTH - snap_image.get_width()) / 2
239     snap_or_miss_rect = pygame.Rect(viewfinder_left + snap_or_miss_border, viewfinder_top,
240                             snap_image.get_width(), snap_image.get_height())
241
242     if snap_visible is True:
243         game_screen.blit(snap_image, snap_or_miss_rect)
244     elif miss_visible is True:
245         game_screen.blit(miss_image, snap_or_miss_rect)
246
247     pygame.display.update()
248     clock.tick(60)
```

Figure 8-6. *Snapper code listing 22*

Insert the Figure 8-6 code at line 237. Take particular care with lines 239–240. This is actually one line of code split over two lines. Key it in exactly as shown, and when you reach the comma at the end of line 239, hit return and continue typing line 240:

- Lines 238–240 work out the dimensions of the rectangle which will hold the snap_image or the miss_image. The tick/cross image will be positioned in the middle of the camera viewfinder.

- Lines 242–246 will display either the snap_image (green tick) if snap_visible is True or the miss_image (red cross) if miss_visible is True. Of course, if neither is True, then neither will be displayed.

Run the game again to see this code in action.

Key learning   Pygame has an event MOUSEBUTTONDOWN which is set when the mouse button is clicked.

The Pygame function colliderect is used to determine if two rectangles have collided.

Step 8: Game over

In Snapper, the game will be over if the player's lives reach zero. At the moment, we have a variable `lives` which is initialized with three at the start of the game and is reduced by one each time the player takes a photo but misses the animal. However, there is nothing in the program code to explain what to do when all the lives have run out. Let's deal with that next. Enter code listing 23 (Figure 8-7).

```
# Check for mouse and key presses
for event in pygame.event.get():

    # Mouse button clicked
    mouse_button_pressed = False
    if event.type == pygame.MOUSEBUTTONDOWN:
        mouse_button_pressed = True

    # Return key pressed when game over
    key_pressed = pygame.key.get_pressed()
    if key_pressed[pygame.K_RETURN] and lives == 0:
        if score > hi_score:
            hi_score = score

        lives = GAME_LIVES
        score = 0

        animal = get_random_animal(animals)
        animal_timer = animal.get('time')
        no_animal_timer = 0

        animal_visible = True

        snap_visible = False
        miss_visible = False

    # User quits
    if event.type == QUIT:
        pygame.quit()
        sys.exit()
```

Figure 8-7. *Snapper code listing 23*

Add the game over code at line 119. Let's take a look at how it works:

- Line 120 gets details of any key presses from the Pygame `get_pressed()` function and stores them in the variable `key_pressed`,
- Line 121 checks for two things:
  - To see if the key pressed was RETURN
  - To see if the number of lives remaining equals zero (in other words, is it game over)

The remaining block of code will run if the game is over and the player has pressed RETURN:

- Lines 122–123 check if the score has beaten the current high score and, if so, set the high score to the game score. We saw this code used in Forest Bomber.

- Lines 125–126 reset the number of `lives` and the `score`.

- Line 128 uses our `get_random_animal` function to get a new random animal.

- Lines 129–130 set up the `animal_timer` and the `no_animal_timer`.

- Finally, lines 132–135 ensure that the animal will be visible and the `snap_image` and `miss_image` are both hidden.

And that's it. A new game is set up ready to go. Run the code to test it. The only thing that's missing is a scoreboard.

Step 9: Scoreboard

In Forest Bomber, we saw how to write code to display a scoreboard. We will use a similar process in Snapper, but this time the scoreboard will be displayed at the bottom of the screen.

In Snapper, we will break our scoreboard code down into two functions:

- `display_scoreboard_data` to display the text on the scoreboard

- `display_game_over` to display the game over message at the end of the game

```
269    # Get a random animal from the dictionary
270    def get_random_animal(animals):
271        random_animal = random.choice(list(animals.keys()))
272        return animals.get(random_animal)
273
274
275    # Handle the text display
276    def display_scoreboard_data(scoreboard_text, alignment):
277        display_text = font.render(scoreboard_text, True, WHITE)
278        text_rect = display_text.get_rect()
279
280        text_loc = [0, 0]
281
282        if alignment == 'Left':
283            text_loc = [SCOREBOARD_MARGIN, SCREEN_HEIGHT - SCOREBOARD_HEIGHT]
284
285        elif alignment == 'Centre':
286            text_loc = [(SCREEN_WIDTH - text_rect.width) / 2, SCREEN_HEIGHT - SCOREBOARD_HEIGHT]
287
288        game_screen.blit(display_text, text_loc)
289
290
291    if __name__ == '__main__':
292        main()
```

Figure 8-8.   *Snapper code listing 24*

First, add the `display_scoreboard_data` function shown in Figure 8-8 at line 276.

```
275    # Handle the text display
276    def display_scoreboard_data(scoreboard_text, alignment):
277        display_text = font.render(scoreboard_text, True, WHITE)
278        text_rect = display_text.get_rect()
279
280        text_loc = [0, 0]
281
282        if alignment == 'Left':
283            text_loc = [SCOREBOARD_MARGIN, SCREEN_HEIGHT - SCOREBOARD_HEIGHT]
284
285        elif alignment == 'Centre':
286            text_loc = [(SCREEN_WIDTH - text_rect.width) / 2, SCREEN_HEIGHT - SCOREBOARD_HEIGHT]
287
288        game_screen.blit(display_text, text_loc)
289
290
291    # Display end of game message
292    def display_game_over():
293
294        game_over_rect = (3 * SCOREBOARD_HEIGHT, 8 * SCOREBOARD_HEIGHT,
295                          SCREEN_WIDTH - SCOREBOARD_HEIGHT * 6, SCOREBOARD_HEIGHT * 5)
296
297        pygame.draw.rect(game_screen, DARK_GREEN, game_over_rect)
298
299        text_line_1 = font.render('GAME OVER', True, WHITE)
300        text_rect_1 = text_line_1.get_rect()
301        text_line_1_loc = [(SCREEN_WIDTH - text_rect_1.width) / 2, (SCREEN_HEIGHT / 2) - 16]
302
303        text_line_2 = font.render('Hit RETURN for a new game', True, WHITE)
304        text_rect_2 = text_line_2.get_rect()
305        text_line_2_loc = [(SCREEN_WIDTH - text_rect_2.width) / 2, (SCREEN_HEIGHT / 2) + 16]
306
307        game_screen.blit(text_line_1, text_line_1_loc)
308        game_screen.blit(text_line_2, text_line_2_loc)
309
310
311    if __name__ == '__main__':
312        main()
```

Figure 8-9.   *Snapper code listing 25*

Next, add the `display_game_over` function at line 291 as shown in Figure 8-9. Note that there are two blank lines separating each function. While the number of blank lines does not affect the program, it makes the program that little easier to read.

We won't look at the code held in these functions in any detail, other than to say that they use math to align and display any text and rectangular boxes on the screen.

It is worth noting that the `display_scoreboard_data` function takes in two parameters:

- Some text which will be stored in the parameter `scoreboard_text`.

- The alignment setting for the text, which will be stored in the parameter `alignment`. The alignment is a string which can be either 'Left' or 'Centre', and this function will align the text accordingly.

A final block of code is needed to make use of these functions and complete the Snapper game.

Add the code from Figure 8-10 at line 265.

```
260        if snap_visible is True:
261            game_screen.blit(snap_image, snap_or_miss_rect)
262        elif miss_visible is True:
263            game_screen.blit(miss_image, snap_or_miss_rect)
264
265        # Display score board
266        score_text = 'Score: ' + str(score)
267        display_scoreboard_data(score_text, 'Left')
268
269        hi_score_text = 'Hi: ' + str(hi_score)
270        display_scoreboard_data(hi_score_text, 'Centre')
271
272        # Display the lives remaining
273        for life in range(1, lives + 1):
274            life_xloc = SCREEN_WIDTH - life * (lives_image.get_width() + 2 * SCOREBOARD_MARGIN)
275            life_y_loc = SCREEN_HEIGHT - SCOREBOARD_HEIGHT
276            game_screen.blit(lives_image, [life_xloc, life_y_loc])
277
278        if lives == 0:
279            display_game_over()
280
281        pygame.display.update()
282        clock.tick(60)
```

Figure 8-10. *Snapper code listing 26*

Notice that we are calling our `display_scoreboard_data` function at line 267 and again at line 270. We call the `display_game_over` function at line 279.

Well done! You have now programmed two games. Don't spend too long playing Snapper though – I hear that planet earth is about be hit by an alien invasion...

## CHAPTER 9

Alien Invasion part 1: Under attack

Commander Jennifer Fisher knew that this code red was no drill. The intermittent bright lights that had been illuminating the Arizona night skies above her military base for the past month meant everyone was on high alert.

But tonight the lights were brighter, almost constant. Tonight the lights were accompanied by a series of high-pitched beeps and a low, almost dizzying hum.

Tonight Commander Fisher could just about make out what appeared to be some kind of spacecraft high in the night sky.

Getting started

Alien Invasion is a space arcade game, where the goal is to prevent earth being invaded by alien Unidentified Flying Objects (UFOs). The player controls a moving base and has 20 missiles to shoot down as many UFOs as possible.

UFOs will move around the upper area of the screen and have the ability to destroy incoming missiles with a special force field defense ray.

© Mark Cunningham 2020
M. Cunningham, *Game Programming with Code Angel,*
https://doi.org/10.1007/978-1-4842-5305-2_9

Let's take a look at the steps involved in making Alien Invasion:

1. Set up the game environment.

2. Initialize variables.

3. Display background.

4. Drive the base.

5. Launch missile.

6. Move UFOs.

7. Shoot UFOs.

8. Game over.

9. Scoreboard.

Again we see that steps 1, 2, 3, 8, and 9 are in common with the previous two games. Steps 4–7 are where the interesting code will happen.

Let's preview the Alien Invasion screen design to get a better idea of how the finished game will look (Figure 9-1).

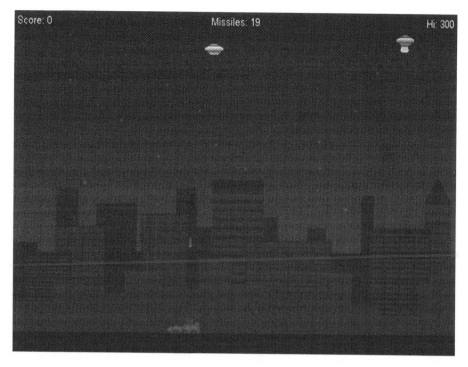

Figure 9-1. *Alien Invasion screen design*

Step 1: Set up the game environment

By now, you will be familiar with the game environment setup. Enter the code shown in Figure 9-2.

```
 1   #!/usr/bin/python
 2   # Alien Invasion
 3   # Code Angel
 4
 5   import sys
 6   import os
 7   import pygame
 8   from pygame.locals import *
 9   import random
10
11   # Define the colours
12   LIGHT_YELLOW = (255, 255, 204)
13   WHITE = (255, 255, 255)
14
15   # Define constants
16   SCREEN_WIDTH = 640
17   SCREEN_HEIGHT = 480
18   SCOREBOARD_MARGIN = 4
19
20   MISSILE_PLATFORM = 31
21   MISSILE_SPEED = 10
22   GAME_MISSILES = 20
23
24   UFO_UPPER_Y = 20
25   UFO_LOWER_Y = 240
26   UFO_HIT_TIME = 20
27   UFO_OFF_TIME = 60
28   UFO_SCORE = 50
29
30   RANDOM_VERTICAL_CHANGE = 20
31   RANDOM_HORIZONTAL_CHANGE = 100
32   UFO_DIRECTIONS = ['left', 'right', 'up', 'down']
33
34   RANDOM_RAY = 200
35   RANDOM_RAY_TIME_MAX = 120
36   RANDOM_RAY_TIME_MIN = 30
37
38   BASE_SPEED = 6
39
```

Figure 9-2. *Alien Invasion code listing 1*

First, we set up the Python and Pygame libraries and declare a number of constants for use in the game.

Let's take a look at some of the more interesting constants:

- MISSILE_SPEED

    The number of pixels that a missile will travel in a frame. Increase this value to make missiles move more quickly.

- GAME_MISSILES

  The total number of missiles in each game. Increase
  this value for a longer game.

- UFO_UPPER_Y, UFO_LOWER_Y

  The UFOs will only fly between these y coordinates.

- BASE_SPEED

  The number of pixels that the base will travel in a
  frame. Increase this value to make the base move faster.

Next, we create a Pygame game environment and load in the images
and audio that will be used in the game. Enter code listing 2 (Figure 9-3).

```
40   # Setup
41   os.environ['SDL_VIDEO_CENTERED'] = '1'
42   pygame.mixer.pre_init(44100, -16, 2, 512)
43   pygame.mixer.init()
44   pygame.init()
45   game_screen = pygame.display.set_mode((SCREEN_WIDTH, SCREEN_HEIGHT))
46   pygame.display.set_caption('Alien Invasion')
47   pygame.key.set_repeat(10, 20)
48   clock = pygame.time.Clock()
49   font = pygame.font.SysFont('Helvetica', 16)
50
51   # Load images
52   background_image = pygame.image.load('background.png').convert()
53   base_image = pygame.image.load('base.png').convert_alpha()
54   missile_image = pygame.image.load('missile.png').convert_alpha()
55   missile_fired_image = pygame.image.load('missile_fired.png').convert_alpha()
56
57   ufo_1_image = pygame.image.load('ufo 1.png').convert_alpha()
58   ufo_2_image = pygame.image.load('ufo 2.png').convert_alpha()
59   ufo_1_exploded_image = pygame.image.load('ufo 1 exploded.png').convert_alpha()
60   ufo_2_exploded_image = pygame.image.load('ufo 2 exploded.png').convert_alpha()
61   ufo_ray_image_1 = pygame.image.load('ufo ray 1.png').convert_alpha()
62   ufo_ray_image_2 = pygame.image.load('ufo ray 2.png').convert_alpha()
63
64   # Load sounds
65   spaceship_hit_sound = pygame.mixer.Sound('spaceship_hit.ogg')
66   launch_sound = pygame.mixer.Sound('launch.ogg')
67
68
```

Figure 9-3. *Alien Invasion code listing 2*

Step 2: Initialize variables

Add code listing 3 (Figure 9-4) to initialize the game variables.

```
69    def main():
70
71        # Initialize variables
72        base_x = 300
73        base_y = 430
74        base_width = base_image.get_rect().width
75
76        ufo_width = ufo_1_image.get_rect().width
77        ufo_height = ufo_1_image.get_rect().height
78
79        ray_width = ufo_ray_image_1.get_rect().width
80
81        ufo_1_x = SCREEN_WIDTH - ufo_width
82        ufo_1_y = random.randint(UFO_UPPER_Y, UFO_LOWER_Y)
83
84        # UFO 1 dictionary
85        ufo_1 = {'x_loc': ufo_1_x, 'y_loc': ufo_1_y, 'direction': 'left', 'hit': False, 'hit_time': 0, 'off_time': 0,
86                 'ray_time': 0, 'speed': 5}
87
88        ufo_2_y = random.randint(UFO_UPPER_Y, UFO_LOWER_Y)
89
90        # UFO 2 dictionary
91        ufo_2 = {'x_loc': 0, 'y_loc': ufo_2_y, 'direction': 'right', 'hit': False, 'hit_time': 0, 'off_time': 0,
92                 'ray_time': 0, 'speed': 3}
93
94        missile_x = 0
95        missile_y = 0
96        missile_firing = False
97
98        missile_width = missile_image.get_rect().width
99        missile_height = missile_image.get_rect().height
100
101       score = 0
102       hi_score = 0
103       missiles = GAME_MISSILES
104       game_over = False
105
```

Figure 9-4. *Alien Invasion code listing 3*

Let's take a look at some of these variables and what they will be used for in the game:

- base_x, base_y

    The location of the base. base_x will change as the player moves left and right, but base_y will remain the same throughout the game because the base does not move up or down.

- `missile_firing`

  A Boolean variable which indicates whether or not a missile has been fired and is on the game screen.

- `ufo_1`, `ufo_2`

  These are dictionaries which store data about each UFO, namely

  - `x_loc`, `y_loc`

    UFO coordinates

  - `direction`

    Direction in which the UFO is travelling

  - `hit`

    Has the UFO been hit or not?

  - `off_time`

    Length of time the UFO spends off-screen after being hit

  - `ray_time`

    Length of time the UFO blaster ray can be operational

  - `speed`

    Speed at which the UFO moves. Notice ufo_1 is faster than ufo_2.

- You should be able to work out the purpose of the variables `score`, `hi_score`, `missiles`, and `game_over` at lines 101–104.

Step 3: Display the background

We saw in both Forest Bomber and Snapper that we can display our game background by using the Pygame blit command to position the background image at coordinates (0,0). We will use the same approach for Alien Invasion.

We also saw in both games that we can use a while True loop to make the game run forever, or at least until the player closes the game window.

Let's add the basic code structure shown in Figure 9-5 to our Alien Invasion program.

```
106    # Main game loop
107    while True:
108
109        for event in pygame.event.get():
110
111            # User quits
112            if event.type == QUIT:
113                pygame.quit()
114                sys.exit()
115
116        # Draw background
117        game_screen.blit(background_image, (0, 0))
118
119        pygame.display.update()
120        clock.tick(30)
121
122
123 if __name__ == '__main__':
124     main()
```

Figure 9-5. *Alien Invasion code listing 4*

Test if the game works by running the code. You should see the game background and be able to quit by closing the game window, but that's all.

In the next chapter, we will write the code to move the base and fire missiles.

CHAPTER 10

Alien Invasion part 2: Missile launch is Go

Commander Fisher stood inside Hangar 21, watching intently as her team of mechanics made the final adjustments to the MM-44 Missile Launch Vehicle (MLV). Her crew had assembled and were awaiting further instruction.

'Get the MLV started Corporal Garcia,' Fisher shouted above the noise that filled the hangar. 'This time we go for real.'

The crew boarded the MLV, the engine burst into life, and Corporal Garcia accelerated through the hangar doors and into the Arizona night.

In this chapter, we will complete the following steps from our game design:

4. Drive the base.

5. Launch missile.

Step 4: Drive the base

The Missile Launch Vehicle is referred to as the base in the game code. The base will move left or right, and movement will be controlled by the arrow keys.

© Mark Cunningham 2020
M. Cunningham, *Game Programming with Code Angel,*
https://doi.org/10.1007/978-1-4842-5305-2_10

```
106     # Main game loop
107     while True:
108
109         for event in pygame.event.get():
110
111             # User quits
112             if event.type == QUIT:
113                 pygame.quit()
114                 sys.exit()
115
116         # Draw background
117         game_screen.blit(background_image, [0, 0])
118
119         pygame.display.update()
120         clock.tick(30)
121
122
123     if __name__ == '__main__':
124         main()
```

Figure 10-1. Alien Invasion code listing 5

Add the code shown in Figure 10-1 at line 112. We have already seen how Pygame stores a list of key press events which can be retrieved by using pygame.key.get_pressed(). As before, we store the key press events in our variable key_pressed.

Looking at this code block

- Line 113 tests to see if the left arrow key was pressed.

- If the left arrow was pressed, line 114 takes the BASE_SPEED constant away from the base's x coordinate. Remember BASE_SPEED is the number of pixels that the base will move in one frame (in our game, BASE_SPEED is set to 6). Also remember we use -= to subtract a value from a variable.

- Line 115 tests to see if the base's x coordinate base_x has gone below 0. If base_x is less than 0, this means the base will have moved off the left-hand edge of the screen. This is not good.

- To resolve this issue, if base_x is less than 0, line 116
  sets base_x to 0. This means that the base can never go
  beyond the left-hand side of the screen.

Lines 119–122 do virtually the same thing as in the preceding text, but
instead move the base right instead of left:

- Line 119 tests to see if the right arrow key was pressed.

- If it was, line 120 adds BASE_SPEED onto base_x.

- Line 121 tests to see if the base has gone beyond the
  right-hand edge of the screen.

- If the base has gone beyond the right-hand edge of the
  screen, line 122 sets the base_x coordinate so that the
  base is flush with the right-hand screen edge.

Of course we can't see anything happening yet because we have not
drawn the base on the screen. Let's do that now. Add the code shown in
Figure 10-2.

```
119     # Draw background
120     game_screen.blit(background_image, [0, 0])
121
122     # Draw base
123     game_screen.blit(base_image, [base_x, base_y])
124
125     pygame.display.update()
126     clock.tick(30)
```

Figure 10-2. *Alien Invasion code listing 6*

Now run Alien Invasion. The base will appear at the foot of the screen
and can be moved left or right using the arrow keys.

Comparison operators

In Python, we can compare two values using *comparison operators*. We
have already encountered some comparison operators in this book. For
example, the code which tests if the base has gone beyond the left-hand

111

side of the screen uses the less than (<) comparison operator, while the code which checks if the base has gone beyond the right-hand side of the screen uses the greater than (>) comparison operator.

This is a good opportunity to review all of the comparison operators that can be used in Python (Table 10-1).

Table 10-1. *Comparison operators*

Comparison Operator	Definition
==	Is equal to
!=	Is not equal to
>	Greater than
<	Less than
>=	Greater than or equal to
<=	Less than or equal to

Step 5: Launch missile

Now that the player is able to drive the base, the next step is to write the code to launch a missile. In the game, a missile will be launched when the spacebar is pressed. Once a missile has been launched, it should not be possible to launch a second missile until the first missile has either disappeared off the top of the screen or hit a UFO. Enter the code shown in Figure 10-3.

```
113        # Right key pressed, move base right
114        elif key_pressed[pygame.K_RIGHT]:
115            base_x += BASE_SPEED
116            if base_x > SCREEN_WIDTH - base_width:
117                base_x = SCREEN_WIDTH - base_width
118
119        # Space pressed, fire missile
120        elif key_pressed[pygame.K_SPACE] and missile_firing is False and game_over is False:
121            missile_firing = True
122            missile_x = base_x + MISSILE_PLATFORM
123            missile_y = base_y - missile_height
124            missiles -= 1
125            launch_sound.play()
126            if missiles == 0:
127                game_over = True
128
129        # User quits
130        if event.type == QUIT:
131            pygame.quit()
132            sys.exit()
```

Figure 10-3. *Alien Invasion code listing 7*

Let's go through this code block line by line:

- Line 125 uses an elif command as an extension of the key_pressed if statement. This time we are testing to see if the key pressed was SPACE. Let's look at the line in detail. There are three separate conditions which all must be met in order for a missile to be fired:

  - The SPACE key has been pressed.

  - missile_firing is False, which means a missile has not already been launched.

  - game_over is False, which means the game is not over.

If all three of these conditions are met, we fire a missile with the code between lines 126 and 132:

- Line 126: Sets the Boolean variable missile_firing to True (this will prevent any other missiles being fired at the same time).

- Line 127: Sets the x coordinate of the missile to start a few pixels to the right of the base_x coordinate (we add on MISSILE_PLATFORM so that the missile launch location is in line with the missile platform).

- Line 128: Sets the y coordinate of the missile so that its starting position is on top of the base.

- Line 129: Reduces the number of missiles in the game by 1.

- Line 130: Plays a fire missile sound effect.

- Lines 131 and 132: Test if the number of missiles has dropped to zero and if so set the game_over Boolean variable to True.

Move the missile

Once the missile has been launched, we need to keep its y coordinate changing; otherwise, it will not actually move. We subtract MISSILE_SPEED from the missile's y coordinate (missile_y).

The code in Figure 10-4 is the code that will do that.

```
134        # User quits
135        if event.type == QUIT:
136            pygame.quit()
137            sys.exit()
138
139        # Update missile location
140        if missile_firing is True:
141            missile_y -= MISSILE_SPEED
142            if missile_y < 0:
143                missile_firing = False
144
145        # Draw background
146        game_screen.blit(background_image, [0, 0])
```

Figure 10-4. *Alien Invasion code listing 8*

- At line 140, we test if the missile_firing variable is True. If it is True, then we know that a missile has been launched and so needs to be moved. The code between lines 141 and 143 will move the missile.

- Line 141 moves the missile upward by the number of pixels held in the constant MISSILE_SPEED.

- Line 142 checks to see if the missile's y coordinate is less than zero. If missile_y < 0, the missile has gone off the top edge of the screen. If that happens, we set missile_firing to False so that the player can launch a new missile.

Display missile

Finally, in order to see the effect of the missile being fired, we need to draw it on the screen. Add code listing 9 (Figure 10-5) to your program.

```
142      # Draw base
143      game_screen.blit(base_image, [base_x, base_y])
144
145      # Draw missile
146      if missile_firing is True:
147          game_screen.blit(missile_fired_image, [missile_x, missile_y])
148      else:
149          game_screen.blit(missile_image, [base_x + MISSILE_PLATFORM, base_y - missile_height])
150
151      pygame.display.update()
152      clock.tick(30)
```

Figure 10-5. *Alien Invasion code listing 9*

There are actually two missile images:

- The first, missile_fired_image, is drawn when missile_firing is True and the missile has been launched.

- The second, missile_image, is drawn when missile_firing is False and the missile is sitting on the top of the base waiting to be launched.

Logical operators

Logical operators are used with conditions (if statements, while loops) to build more complex conditions.

There are three logical operators:

- and

- or

- not

Let's look at a simple if condition for a moment, one that we used back in the Snapper program:

```
if lives == 0:
    display_game_over()
```

In this example, lives == 0 is known as an operand. An operand will evaluate to either true (if lives equal 0) or false (if lives are not equal to 0).

We can use *logical operators* to join more than one operand to make a complex condition.

For example, we used the **and** logical operator when deciding whether or not to launch a missile. Look back to line 125, the elif statement

```
elif key_pressed[pygame.K_SPACE] and
missile_firing is False and
game_over is False:
```

The **and** logical operator is used here to ensure that each of the three operands evaluates to true before launching the missile. The missile can only be launched if

- The space key has been pressed:

  ```
  key_pressed[pygame.K_SPACE]
  ```

- The missile has not already been fired:

  ```
  missile_firing is False
  ```

- The game is not over:

  `game_over is False`

Table 10-2 shows each of the three logical operators.

Table 10-2. Logical operators

Operator	Definition	Example
and	True if both operands evaluate to true	a and b
or	True if either of the operands evaluates to true	a or b
not	True if the operand evaluates to false	not a

We will see an example of the or logical operator in the next chapter.

But for now, let's get back to Alien Invasion. We have a missile launcher which we can move left and right, and we can fire missiles, but there don't seem to be any aliens invading planet earth. At least not yet anyway...

CHAPTER 11

Alien Invasion part 3: And they came from outer space

Commander Fisher peered through her binoculars, focusing on the dark sky above. She could clearly make out two large elliptical objects, their metallic exterior reflecting the luminous light of the moon. There was no doubt that these Unidentified Flying Objects were getting steadily closer to planet earth.

Fisher had already received her orders from her commanding officer. Attempts had been made to communicate with the extraterrestrial spaceships, but with no success. The decision had been taken – earth was under attack, and Fisher and her crew were to do all in their power to defend the planet.

Commander Fisher put down the binoculars and turned to Corporal Garcia.

'Prepare to launch, as soon as I give the word.'

In this chapter, we will move the UFOs around the game screen completing step 6.

© Mark Cunningham 2020
M. Cunningham, *Game Programming with Code Angel*,
https://doi.org/10.1007/978-1-4842-5305-2_11

Step 6: Move UFOs

As there are two UFOs in the game, it makes sense to write a single function to move them rather than repeat the code twice.

Figure 11-1 shows the code for the move_ufo function. When entering the code, use two line spaces above and below the function.

```
        pygame.display.update()
        clock.tick(30)


# Move the UFO
def move_ufo(ufo, ufo_width):
    if ufo.get('hit') is False:
        if ufo.get('direction') == 'left':
            ufo['x_loc'] -= ufo.get('speed')
        elif ufo.get('direction') == 'right':
            ufo['x_loc'] += ufo.get('speed')
        elif ufo.get('direction') == 'up':
            ufo['y_loc'] -= ufo.get('speed')
        elif ufo.get('direction') == 'down':
            ufo['y_loc'] += ufo.get('speed')

        # If the UFO goes off the screen left, reset x coordinate and change direction
        if ufo.get('x_loc') < 0:
            ufo['x_loc'] = 0
            ufo['direction'] = 'right'

        # If the UFO goes off the screen right, reset x coordinate and change direction
        elif ufo.get('x_loc') > SCREEN_WIDTH - ufo_width:
            ufo['x_loc'] = SCREEN_WIDTH - ufo_width
            ufo['direction'] = 'left'

        # If the UFO goes too high, reset y coordinate and change direction
        elif ufo.get('y_loc') < UFO_UPPER_Y:
            ufo['y_loc'] = UFO_UPPER_Y
            ufo['direction'] = 'down'

        # If the UFO goes too low, reset y coordinate and change direction
        elif ufo.get('y_loc') > UFO_LOWER_Y:
            ufo['y_loc'] = UFO_LOWER_Y
            ufo['direction'] = 'up'

        # If none of the above, then random chance of changing direction
        else:
            if ufo.get('direction') == 'up' or ufo.get('direction') == 'down':
                ufo_direction_chance = random.randint(0, RANDOM_VERTICAL_CHANGE)
            else:
                ufo_direction_chance = random.randint(0, RANDOM_HORIZONTAL_CHANGE)

            if ufo_direction_chance == 1:
                ufo['direction'] = random.choice(UFO_DIRECTIONS)


if __name__ == '__main__':
    main()
```

Figure 11-1. *Alien Invasion code listing 10*

The function takes two parameters:

- The ufo dictionary which was initialized earlier in the game

- The ufo width

There seems like quite a lot of code in the move_ufo function, but most of it is fairly straightforward. Let's examine it in more detail.

To understand how move_ufo works, we need first to remind ourselves what data the UFO dictionary holds. In particular, we are interested in the following keys:

- x_loc: The x coordinate of the UFO

- y_loc: The y coordinate of the UFO

- direction: The direction in which the UFO is moving (left, right, up, or down)

- speed: The number of pixels that the UFO will move in a single frame (remember ufo_1 has a greater speed than ufo_2)

- hit: A Boolean value which will be True if the UFO has been hit by a missile and False if it has not

Before we move the UFO, we test the dictionary key hit. We will only move the UFO if the value of hit is False. In other words, we will not move the UFO if it has been hit by a missile.

Lines 164–171 move the UFO by changing the value of its x or y coordinate by the value of its speed. The multiline if statement is used to calculate the direction in which the UFO is moving, and from that the code decides whether to add or subtract the speed from the x or y coordinate.

For example

- Line 164 tests if the direction is left, and if it is, line 165 subtracts the speed from the x coordinate.

- Line 170 tests if the direction is down, and if it is, line 171 adds the speed onto the y coordinate.

Stay on screen

Remember when we wrote the code to drive the missile launcher, we made sure that it would not drive off the edge of the screen? We will do the same thing with our UFOs.

- Lines 174–181 check to see if the UFO has reached the left or right edge of the screen. If it has, it reverses the UFO direction so that it will head the other way.

- Lines 184–191 do almost the same thing, except instead of the edge of the screen, we use two constant variables UFO_UPPER_Y and UFO_LOWER._Y. These are initialized at the start of the program and are used to keep both of the UFOs in an upper area of the screen.

  For example, if the UFO is moving up and its y coordinate becomes less than UFO_UPPER_Y, we set the y coordinate to UFO_UPPER_Y and then change the direction to 'down'.

  Similarly, if the UFO is moving down and its y coordinate becomes greater than UFO_LOWER_Y, we set the y coordinate to UFO_LOWER_Y and then change the direction to 'up'.

Time for a change

Next, we will concentrate on the else statement on line 154 and the block of code below it. This else statement will only be reached if the UFO did not go off the edge of the screen. In this code block, we will throw in some random movement changes to make the game more interesting and challenging.

First, we need to understand the purpose of the two constants that are used by the code:

- RANDOM_VERTICAL_CHANGE: The chances of a change in direction if the UFO is moving up/down. This is set to 20 at the start of the game.

- RANDOM_HORIZONTAL_CHANGE: The chances of a change in direction if the UFO is moving left/right. This is set to 100 at the start of the game.

Line 195 tests to see if the UFO is moving up or down. Notice we have used the **or** conditional operator that we described in the previous chapter.

If the UFO is moving up or down, line 196 sets the variable ufo_direction_chance to a random number between 1 and 20.

If the UFO is not moving up or down, then it must be moving left or right. In this case, line 198 sets the variable ufo_direction_chance to a random number between 1 and 100.

Finally, line 200 tests to see if the random ufo_direction_chance equals 1. If ufo_direction_chance equals 1, we change direction by picking a random direction from the list of four UFO directions (left, right, up, down).

In summary, during each frame, there is

- A 1 in 20 chance of a change in direction if the UFO is moving up or down.

- A 1 in 100 chance of a change in direction if the UFO is moving left or right.

Call the function

We have written the move_ufo function, but nothing will happen yet because it does not get called by the main program.

```
139    # Update missile location
140    if missile_firing is True:
141        missile_y -= MISSILE_SPEED
142        if missile_y < 0:
143            missile_firing = False
144
145    # Update UFO locations
146    move_ufo(ufo_1, ufo_width)
147    move_ufo(ufo_2, ufo_width)
148
149    # Draw background
150    game_screen.blit(background_image, [0, 0])
```

Figure 11-2. *Alien Invasion code listing 11*

Add the code shown in Figure 11-2 at line 145 which calls the move_ufo function for each of the UFOs.

Display UFOs

Finally, we need to blit the two UFOs onto the screen.

```
155    # Draw missile
156    if missile_firing is True:
157        game_screen.blit(missile_fired_image, [missile_x, missile_y])
158    else:
159        game_screen.blit(missile_image, [base_x + MISSILE_PLATFORM, base_y - missile_height])
160
161    # Draw UFOs
162    if ufo_1.get('hit_time') > 0:
163        game_screen.blit(ufo_1_exploded_image, [ufo_1.get('x_loc'), ufo_1.get('y_loc')])
164    elif ufo_1.get('hit') is False:
165        game_screen.blit(ufo_1_image, [ufo_1.get('x_loc'), ufo_1.get('y_loc')])
166
167    if ufo_2.get('hit_time') > 0:
168        game_screen.blit(ufo_2_exploded_image, [ufo_2.get('x_loc'), ufo_2.get('y_loc')])
169    elif ufo_2.get('hit') is False:
170        game_screen.blit(ufo_2_image, [ufo_2.get('x_loc'), ufo_2.get('y_loc')])
171
172    pygame.display.update()
173    clock.tick(30)
```

Figure 11-3. *Alien Invasion code listing 12*

The code shown in Figure 11-3 which displays each UFO is just a bit more complicated than usual:

- At line 162 (and 167), we test to see if the hit_time key in the UFO dictionary is greater than 0. If the UFO has a hit time, it means it has been hit by a missile, and hit_time is a countdown timer. In this case, we should display an exploded UFO image.

- At line 164 (and 169), we test to see if the hit key in the UFO dictionary is False. We will only display the UFO image if hit is False, that is, the UFO has not been hit by a missile.

Run the game. If you have written the code correctly, you should see two UFOs buzzing about the screen. You can try to shoot them, but nothing will happen if a missile hits them. At least, not yet...

CHAPTER 12

Save the planet

They were getting much closer now, and in a few seconds Commander Fisher knew that the UFOs which she had been monitoring for the past 20 minutes would be in range of the MLV.

She took a breath. 'Wait...' she whispered to no one in particular. 'Wait...'

She knew that it was her time. Everything came down to this.

'Launch missile 1!'

The first missile sped from the launcher lighting up the night sky like an enormous firework. Fisher knew instantly that the projectile was on target. As it shot toward the spaceship she felt sure it would be a direct hit.

And then, seemingly out of nowhere a defense field appeared around the spaceship and the missile exploded before making contact.

Commander Fisher knew that she had only 19 missiles remaining with which to save planet earth.

In this final part of Alien Invasion, we will write the code to shoot the UFOs and complete the game:

7.   Shoot UFOs.

8.   Game over.

9.   Scoreboard.

© Mark Cunningham 2020
M. Cunningham, *Game Programming with Code Angel*,
https://doi.org/10.1007/978-1-4842-5305-2_12

Step 7: Shoot UFOs

We will begin by writing the function shown in Figure 12-1 which will determine if a UFO has been hit.

```
            if ufo_direction_change == 1:
                ufo['direction'] = random.choice(UFO_DIRECTIONS)


# Has the UFO been hit by the missile
def check_ufo_hit(ufo, missile_rect, ufo_width, ufo_height):

    ufo_rect = pygame.Rect(ufo.get('x_loc'), ufo.get('y_loc'), ufo_width, ufo_height)

    if missile_rect.colliderect(ufo_rect):

        # If the missile collides with the UFO and there is no defence ray, direct hit
        if ufo.get('ray_time') == 0:
            ufo_hit = 'direct hit'

        # If the missile collides with the UFO and there is a defence ray, missile is destroyed
        else:
            ufo_hit = 'missile destroyed'

    # If the missile has not collided with the UFO, no hit
    else:
        ufo_hit = 'no hit'

    return ufo_hit


if __name__ == '__main__':
    main()
```

Figure 12-1. *Alien Invasion code listing 13*

The function is passed four parameters:

- `ufo`: The UFO dictionary
- `missile_rect`: The rectangle representing the missile
- `ufo_width`, `ufo_height`: Dimensions of the UFO

The function will return a message back to the main program to indicate whether or not the missile hit the UFO. There are three possible messages:

- `'direct hit'`: The missile has hit the UFO.
- `'missile destroyed'`: The missile hit the UFO, but the UFO had its protective defense ray enabled.
- `'no hit'`: The missile has not hit the UFO.

Line 222 builds a Pygame rectangle which represents the UFO.

Line 224 uses the Pygame `colliderect` function to determine whether or not the missile rectangle has collided with the UFO rectangle.

If the missile has collided with the UFO, then it will register a direct hit if the UFO's `ray_time` value is equal to zero (i.e., it has no defense ray). If `ray_time` is not zero, then the UFO has initiated its defense ray, and the missile will be destroyed before it can hit the UFO.

Next, we must write some code to call this function and to handle the direct hit/missile destroyed scenarios. Enter code listing 14 as shown in Figure 12-2.

```
145       # Update UFO locations
146       move_ufo(ufo_1, ufo_width)
147       move_ufo(ufo_2, ufo_width)
148
149       # Check if missile hits a UFO
150       missile_rect = pygame.Rect(missile_x, missile_y, missile_width, missile_height)
151
152       if ufo_1.get('hit') is False and missile_firing is True:
153           ufo_hit = check_ufo_hit(ufo_1, missile_rect, ufo_width, ufo_height)
154           if ufo_hit == 'missile destroyed':
155               missile_firing = False
156               pygame.mixer.stop()
157
158           elif ufo_hit == 'direct hit':
159               missile_firing = False
160               score += UFO_SCORE * 2
161               ufo_1['hit_time'] = UFO_HIT_TIME
162               ufo_1['hit'] = True
163
164               pygame.mixer.stop()
165               spaceship_hit_sound.play()
166
167       if ufo_2.get('hit') is False and missile_firing is True:
168           ufo_hit = check_ufo_hit(ufo_2, missile_rect, ufo_width, ufo_height)
169           if ufo_hit == 'missile destroyed':
170               missile_firing = False
171               pygame.mixer.stop()
172
173           elif ufo_hit == 'direct hit':
174               missile_firing = False
175               score += UFO_SCORE
176               ufo_2['hit_time'] = UFO_HIT_TIME
177               ufo_2['hit'] = True
178
179               pygame.mixer.stop()
180               spaceship_hit_sound.play()
181
182       # Draw background
183       game_screen.blit(background_image, (0, 0))
```

Figure 12-2. *Alien Invasion code listing 14*

There is quite a bit of code here, but hopefully you can see that lines 152–165 deal with the ufo_1, while lines 167–180 are for ufo_2. Given these are broadly the same, we will only review the code for ufo_1.

Line 152 tests to make sure that

- The value of 'hit' in the UFO dictionary is False – the UFO has not been hit.

- missile_firing is True – a missile has been fired.

If both of these operands are true, then we call the check_ufo_hit function at line 153. Remember this function will return one of three possible values:

- 'missile_destroyed'

- 'direct_hit'

- 'no_hit'

The value returned by the function will be assigned to the variable ufo_hit.

If the message returned is 'missile_destroyed'

- Line 155 sets missile_firing to False which will stop the missile being displayed on screen (see line 189 – the missile is only displayed if missile_firing is True).

- Line 156 calls pygame.mixer.stop(). This slightly unusual instruction tells Pygame to stop any audio that is currently being played. Because the missile has been destroyed, we need to stop playing the missile's sound effect.

If the message returned is 'direct hit'

- Line 159 sets missile_firing to False to stop the missile being displayed on screen.

- Line 160 adds 2 × the UFO_SCORE value to the current game score. Note that for ufo_2, line 176 adds 1 × UFO_SCORE to the score. This is because ufo_1 moves more quickly and so is harder to hit than ufo_2.

- Line 161 updates the dictionary value hit_time with the constant UFO_HIT_TIME. We will learn later in this chapter that 'hit_time' is a timer used to measure the length of time the UFO should remain on screen in its exploded state.

- Line 162 sets the dictionary value 'hit' to True to indicate that the UFO has been hit.

- Finally, line 164 stops the missile sound effect from playing and plays the audio file which indicates that the spaceship has been hit.

If you run the code now, you will see some minor improvements when a UFO has been hit by a missile, but there is still some work to be done. We are going to add another function update_hit_ufo as shown in Figure 12-3. As ever, remember to use double spacing between functions.

```
            # If the missile has not collided with the UFO, no hit
            else:
                ufo_hit = 'no hit'

            return ufo_hit


# Update status of UFO if it has been hit
def update_hit_ufo(ufo, new_x_loc, new_direction):

    # UFO has been hit, reduce the hit timer
    if ufo.get('hit_time') > 0:
        ufo['hit_time'] -= 1

        # When hit time reaches zero, UFO should go off screen
        if ufo.get('hit_time') == 0:
            ufo['off_time'] = UFO_OFF_TIME

    # UFO is off screen, reduce the off screen time
    elif ufo.get('off_time') > 0:
        ufo['off_time'] -= 1

        # When off screen time reaches 0, set new UFO location and direction
        if ufo.get('off_time') == 0:
            ufo['y_loc'] = random.randint(UFO_UPPER_Y, UFO_LOWER_Y)
            ufo['x_loc'] = new_x_loc
            ufo['direction'] = new_direction
            ufo['hit'] = False


if __name__ == '__main__':
    main()
```

Figure 12-3. *Alien Invasion code listing 15*

131

There are two timers used in this function:

- The hit_time timer counts down the length of time the UFO should be shown on screen in its exploded state. Once hit_time counts down to zero, a second timer off_time is started.

- The off_time timer measures the length of time that the UFO should remain off-screen, until it is respawned by lines 291–294.

Of course, we still have to add the code which will call this function from our main program. It gets called twice, once for each UFO. Add code listing 16 (Figure 12-4) to your program.

```
elif ufo_hit == 'direct hit':
    missile_firing = False
    score += UFO_SCORE
    ufo_2['hit_time'] = UFO_HIT_TIME
    ufo_2['hit'] = True

    pygame.mixer.stop()
    spaceship_hit_sound.play()

# Update hit UFOs
update_hit_ufo(ufo_1, SCREEN_WIDTH - ufo_width, 'left')
update_hit_ufo(ufo_2, 0, 'right')

# Draw background
game_screen.blit(background_image, [0, 0])
```

Figure 12-4. *Alien Invasion code listing 16*

Run the program again; and you should find that when a UFO is hit by a missile, it explodes for a short time, disappears briefly, and then respawns.

Catching some rays

It feels like we have a pretty decent game here now. It's difficult, without being too difficult. There are some random elements which means the player cannot predict what the UFOs are going to do next. To make the game just that little bit harder, we will give each UFO a force field which can destroy a missile. In the code, we will call this force field a ray.

```
262        if ufo_direction_chance == 1:
263            ufo['direction'] = random.choice(UFO_DIRECTIONS)
264
265
266    # Update the status of the UFO ray
267    def update_ray(ufo):
268
269        # If there is not already a ray, then random chance of there being a ray
260        if ufo.get('ray_time') == 0 and ufo.get('hit') is False:
261            random_ray = random.randint(0, RANDOM_RAY)
262            if random_ray == 1:
263                ufo['ray_time'] = random.randint(RANDOM_RAY_TIME_MIN, RANDOM_RAY_TIME_MAX)
264
265        # If there is a ray, decrease its time
266        elif ufo.get('ray_time') > 0:
267            ufo['ray_time'] -= 1
268
269
270    # Has the UFO been hit by the missile
271    def check_ufo_hit(ufo, missile_rect, ufo_width, ufo_height):
272
273        ufo_rect = pygame.Rect(ufo.get('x_loc'), ufo.get('y_loc'), ufo_width, ufo_height)
```

Figure 12-5. *Alien Invasion code listing 17*

Add the function update_ray (Figure 12-5) to the program code. The function works like this:

If the ray_time is zero (there is not already a defense ray), and the UFO has not already been hit (line 260)

- Line 261: Generates a random number between 1 and RANDOM_RAY (set at the start of the program to 200)

- Line 262: If the randomly generated number equals 1

- Line 263: Generates a random ray_time between RANDOM_RAY_TIME_MIN and RANDOM_RAY_TIME_MAX (set at the start of the program to 30 and 120, respectively).

Otherwise, if there is already a ray_time (line 266)

- Line 267: Reduces the ray_time value by 1. Remember, ray_time is a countdown timer for the defense ray.

Of course, we still need to call the function from the main program which we do as shown in Figure 12-6.

```
145    # Update UFO locations
146    move_ufo(ufo_1, ufo_width)
147    move_ufo(ufo_2, ufo_width)
148
149    # Update UFO rays
150    update_ray(ufo_1)
151    update_ray(ufo_2)
152
153    # Check if missile hits a UFO
154    missile_rect = pygame.Rect(missile_x, missile_y, missile_width, missile_height)
```

Figure 12-6. *Alien Invasion code listing 18*

You may already have worked out that this code by itself doesn't do much other than change the value of the UFO dictionary `ray_time`.

We need to add the code shown in Figure 12-7 to the main program to actually display the rays on screen.

```
198    # Draw UFOs
199    if ufo_1.get('hit_time') > 0:
200        game_screen.blit(ufo_1_exploded_image, [ufo_1.get('x_loc'), ufo_1.get('y_loc')])
201    elif ufo_1.get('hit') is False:
202        game_screen.blit(ufo_1_image, [ufo_1.get('x_loc'), ufo_1.get('y_loc')])
203
204    if ufo_2.get('hit_time') > 0:
205        game_screen.blit(ufo_2_exploded_image, [ufo_2.get('x_loc'), ufo_2.get('y_loc')])
206    elif ufo_2.get('hit') is False:
207        game_screen.blit(ufo_2_image, [ufo_2.get('x_loc'), ufo_2.get('y_loc')])
208
209    # Draw UFO defence rays
210    if ufo_1.get('ray_time') > 0:
211        ray_x = ufo_1.get('x_loc') + (ufo_width - ray_width) / 2
212        ray_y = ufo_1.get('y_loc') + ufo_height
213        if ufo_1.get('ray_time') % 4 == 0 or ufo_1.get('ray_time') % 5 == 0:
214            game_screen.blit(ufo_ray_image_2, [ray_x, ray_y])
215        else:
216            game_screen.blit(ufo_ray_image_1, [ray_x, ray_y])
217
218    if ufo_2.get('ray_time') > 0:
219        ray_x = ufo_2.get('x_loc') + (ufo_width - ray_width) / 2
220        ray_y = ufo_2.get('y_loc') + ufo_height
221        if ufo_2.get('ray_time') % 4 == 0 or ufo_2.get('ray_time') % 5 == 0:
222            game_screen.blit(ufo_ray_image_2, [ray_x, ray_y])
223        else:
224            game_screen.blit(ufo_ray_image_1, [ray_x, ray_y])
225
226    pygame.display.update()
227    clock.tick(30)
```

Figure 12-7. *Alien Invasion code listing 19*

We don't really want to get into the detail of this code, other than to say that if the UFO `ray_time` > 0, then it will draw one of the ray images directly below the spaceship.

Run the program now, and you will see that the UFOs produce the defense rays at random. If you shoot a missile at a UFO when its rays are active, the missile will be destroyed.

Step 8: Game over

The game over process will be very similar to Snapper and Forest Bomber, but this time we will write a `display_game_over` function to display an appropriate message. This function is shown in Figure 12-8.

```
# When off screen time reaches 0, set new UFO location and direction
if ufo.get('off_time') == 0:
    ufo['y_loc'] = random.randint(UFO_UPPER_Y, UFO_LOWER_Y)
    ufo['x_loc'] = new_x_loc
    ufo['direction'] = new_direction
    ufo['hit'] = False

# Display the game over message
def display_game_over():
    text_line_1 = font.render('GAME OVER', True, WHITE)
    text_rect_1 = text_line_1.get_rect()
    text_line_1_loc = ((SCREEN_WIDTH - text_rect_1.width) / 2, (SCREEN_HEIGHT / 2) - 16)

    text_line_2 = font.render('Hit RETURN for new game', True, WHITE)
    text_rect_2 = text_line_2.get_rect()
    text_line_2_loc = ((SCREEN_WIDTH - text_rect_2.width) / 2, (SCREEN_HEIGHT / 2) + 16)

    game_screen.blit(text_line_1, text_line_1_loc)
    game_screen.blit(text_line_2, text_line_2_loc)

if __name__ == '__main__':
    main()
```

Figure 12-8. *Alien Invasion code listing 20*

Next, we need to add some code which will display the game over message if the game has finished. Add code listing 21 to your program (Figure 12-9).

```
if ufo_2.get('ray_time') > 0:
    ray_x = ufo_2.get('x_loc') + (ufo_width - ray_width) / 2
    ray_y = ufo_2.get('y_loc') + ufo_height
    if ufo_2.get('ray_time') % 4 == 0 or ufo_2.get('ray_time') % 5 == 0:
        game_screen.blit(ufo_ray_image_2, [ray_x, ray_y])
    else:
        game_screen.blit(ufo_ray_image_1, [ray_x, ray_y])

# Game over
if game_over is True and missile_firing is False:
    if score > hi_score:
        hi_score = score

    display_game_over()

pygame.display.update()
clock.tick(30)
```

Figure 12-9. *Alien Invasion code listing 21*

The Boolean variable game_over gets set to True when all of the missiles have been fired. The reason we check missile_firing is that we need the last missile to either hit a UFO or go off the screen before finishing the game.

We have seen lines 232 and 233 in both of the previous games, and line 235 will call our game_over_function.

Test that game over works by firing 20 missiles, after which the message should be displayed.

However, hitting the return key at the end of the game does nothing. Let's fix that. Add the code shown in Figure 12-10 to the program.

```
# Space pressed, fire missile
elif key_pressed[pygame.K_SPACE] and missile_firing is False and game_over is False:
    missile_firing = True
    missile_x = base_x + MISSILE_PLATFORM
    missile_y = base_y - missile_height
    missiles -= 1
    launch_sound.play()
    if missiles == 0:
        game_over = True

# Return pressed at end of game, start new game
elif key_pressed[pygame.K_RETURN] and game_over is True:
    game_over = False
    score = 0
    missiles = GAME_MISSILES

# User quits
if event.type == QUIT:
    pygame.quit()
    sys.exit()
```

Figure 12-10. *Alien Invasion code listing 22*

By now, it should be fairly obvious what this code does. We test to see if our key_pressed list contains the return key. If it does and the game_over Boolean is True, we reset the three variables game_over, score, and missiles which will start a new game.

Test that the game over process works correctly now.

Step 9: Scoreboard

The last thing we need to do to complete the game is display a scoreboard at the top of the screen. We have seen how to do this in both the previous programs, so it shouldn't require too much explanation.

Add the function `display_scoreboard_data` as shown in Figure 12-11.

```
341         # When off screen time reaches 0, set new UFO location and direction
342         if ufo.get('off_time') == 0:
343             ufo['y_loc'] = random.randint(UFO_UPPER_Y, UFO_LOWER_Y)
344             ufo['x_loc'] = new_x_loc
345             ufo['direction'] = new_direction
346             ufo['hit'] = False
347
348
349     # Display the scoreboard data
350     def display_scoreboard_data(scoreboard_text, alignment):
351         display_text = font.render(scoreboard_text, True, LIGHT_YELLOW)
352         text_rect = display_text.get_rect()
353
354         text_loc = [0, 0]
355
356         if alignment == 'left':
357             text_loc = [SCOREBOARD_MARGIN, SCOREBOARD_MARGIN]
358
359         elif alignment == 'right':
360             text_loc = [SCREEN_WIDTH - text_rect.width - SCOREBOARD_MARGIN, SCOREBOARD_MARGIN]
361
362         elif alignment == 'centre':
363             text_loc = [(SCREEN_WIDTH - text_rect.width) / 2, SCOREBOARD_MARGIN]
364
365         game_screen.blit(display_text, text_loc)
366
367
368     # Display the game over message
369     def display_game_over():
370         text_line_1 = font.render('GAME OVER', True, WHITE)
371         text_rect_1 = text_line_1.get_rect()
372         text_line_1_loc = [(SCREEN_WIDTH - text_rect_1.width) / 2, (SCREEN_HEIGHT / 2) - 16]
```

Figure 12-11. *Alien Invasion code listing 23*

Finally, we add some code to call the scoreboard function as shown in Figure 12-12.

```
# Game over
if game_over is True and missile_firing is False:
    if score > hi_score:
        hi_score = score

    display_game_over()

# Display score board
score_text = 'Score: ' + str(score)
display_scoreboard_data(score_text, 'left')

missile_text = 'Missiles: ' + str(missiles)
display_scoreboard_data(missile_text, 'centre')

hi_score_text = 'Hi: ' + str(hi_score)
display_scoreboard_data(hi_score_text, 'right')

pygame.display.update()
clock.tick(30)
```

Figure 12-12. *Alien Invasion code listing 24*

And there we have it. Three hundred and ninety-three∗ lines of code later, we have our Alien Invasion game!

∗Actually although the listing runs to 393 lines, if you take out all of the line breaks, it's actually only 300, but still…

CHAPTER 13

Golf part 1: On the tee

'So here we are in Scotland, the home of golf, on the final day of The Open. Just three holes stand between this final pair of players and glory. Jim, what's your take on the events that are about to unfold today?'

'It's neck and neck between Mitch Johnson and Tommy Miller here, Corey. I couldn't possibly pick a winner from these two...'

Getting started

If you have made it this far, then well done! And of course, you know what's coming next. We have 100 lines of initialization and setup code before we can get into the game proper. OK, let's just roll our sleeves up and crack on with it.

The idea behind Golf is simple. Get the ball from the tee to the hole in as few strokes as possible. For each hole, the flag will be placed a random distance from the tee, and the player should work out how hard to hit the ball using a power meter/slider. The player will play three holes of golf in a single game.

As with previous projects, let's list the steps required to build the game of Golf:

1. Set up the game environment.

2. Initialize variables.

© Mark Cunningham 2020
M. Cunningham, *Game Programming with Code Angel,*
https://doi.org/10.1007/978-1-4842-5305-2_13

3. Display background.

4. Display flag.

5. Power meter.

6. Move the ball.

7. In the hole.

8. Scoreboard.

Figure 13-1 shows how the screen will look.

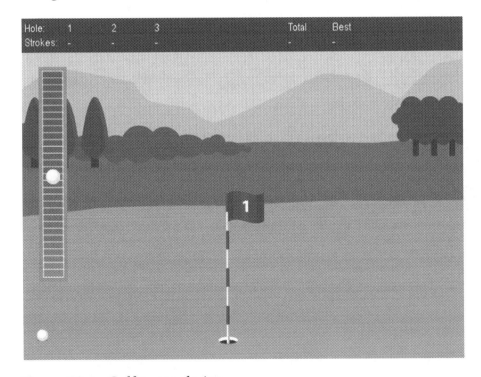

Figure 13-1. *Golf screen design*

Step 1: Set up the game environment

As with the previous games we will begin with the game setup. Enter code listing 1 (Figure 13-2).

```
1    #!/usr/bin/python
2    # Golf
3    # Code Angel
4
5
6    import sys
7    import os
8    import pygame
9    from pygame.locals import *
10   import random
11
12   # Define the colours
13   WHITE = (255, 255, 255)
14   GREY = (62, 87, 113)
15
16   # Define constants
17   SCREEN_WIDTH = 640
18   SCREEN_HEIGHT = 480
19
20   SCOREBOARD_MARGIN = 4
21   SCOREBOARD_HEIGHT = 48
22   SCOREBOARD_LINE = 20
23   SCOREBOARD_COLUMNS = 10
24
25   HOLE_MESSAGE_Y = 60
26
27   METER_X = 25
28   METER_Y = SCOREBOARD_HEIGHT + 20
29
30   SLIDER_BORDER = 5
31   SLIDER_X = 35
32   SLIDER_TOP_PADDDING = 8
33
34   SLIDER_SPEED = 5
35   SLOW_SLIDER_SPEED = 20
36   SLOW_PUTT_RANGE = 3
37
38   MAX_POWER = 30
39   MIN_POWER = 1
40
41   START_BALL_X = 20
42   BALL_Y = 436
43   BALL_STEP = 3
44   BALL_DESCENT = 5
45
46   FLAG_Y = 244
47   RANDOM_FLAG_MIN = 10
48   RANDOM_FLAG_MAX = 30
49   FLAG_STEP = 18
50   HOLE_CENTRE = 8
51
```

Figure 13-2. *Golf code listing 1*

While the setup of the constant variables is not the most interesting part of writing a game, it's worth taking a moment just to review the purpose of some of the more interesting constants we will be using:

- SLIDER_SPEED/SLOW_SLIDER_SPEED: The speeds that the slider moves up and down the meter. There are two speeds because the slider slows down when it is at the bottom of the meter.

- SLOW_PUTT_RANGE: The number of steps on the meter that the power indicator will move at the SLOW_SLIDER_ SPEED. Increasing this number will make the game easier.

- BALL_STEP: The number of pixels that the golf ball moves each frame.

- RANDOM_FLAG_MIN/RANDOM_FLAG_MAX: The range of random flag placements. The tee is at position 1, and the flag can be placed anywhere from position 18 to position 30.

The remainder of the constants relate to pixel coordinates or distances so that the different screen elements can be positioned correctly.

```
52    # Setup
53    os.environ['SDL_VIDEO_CENTERED'] = '1'
54    pygame.mixer.pre_init(44100, -16, 2, 512)
55    pygame.mixer.init()
56    pygame.init()
57    game_screen = pygame.display.set_mode((SCREEN_WIDTH, SCREEN_HEIGHT))
58    pygame.display.set_caption('Golf')
59    clock = pygame.time.Clock()
60    font = pygame.font.SysFont('Helvetica', 16)
61
62    # Load images
63    background_image = pygame.image.load('golf_background.png').convert()
64    power_meter_image = pygame.image.load('power_meter.png').convert()
65    slider_image = pygame.image.load('slider.png').convert_alpha()
66    ball_image = pygame.image.load('ball.png').convert_alpha()
67
68    flag_1_image = pygame.image.load('flag_1.png').convert_alpha()
69    flag_2_image = pygame.image.load('flag_2.png').convert_alpha()
70    flag_3_image = pygame.image.load('flag_3.png').convert_alpha()
71
72    # Load sounds
73    putt_sound = pygame.mixer.Sound('putt.ogg')
74    clap_sound = pygame.mixer.Sound('clap.ogg')
75
76
```

Figure 13-3. *Golf code listing 2*

Enter the code which sets up the Pygame environment and loads in the images and audio (Figure 13-3).

Step 2: Initialize variables

Now add the code shown in Figure 13-4 which initializes some of the variables that we will use in Golf.

```
def main():

    # Initialize variables
    slider_direction = 'up'
    slider_timer = SLOW_SLIDER_SPEED
    shot_power = 1
    meter_height = power_meter_image.get_rect().height - 2 * SLIDER_BORDER

    ball_x = START_BALL_X
    ball_distance = 0
    ball_direction = 'right'
    final_ball_location = 0
    moves_per_flag = FLAG_STEP / BALL_STEP

    flag_distance = random.randint(RANDOM_FLAG_MIN, RANDOM_FLAG_MAX)
    flag_x = flag_distance * FLAG_STEP + HOLE_CENTRE

    hole = 1

    hole_strokes = [0, 0, 0]
    round_strokes = 0
    best_round_strokes = 0

    in_the_hole = False
```

Figure 13-4. Golf code listing 3

Let's take a moment to review some of the more important variables:

- slider_direction: The direction in which the ball on the slider moves. slider_direction is a string variable which can be either 'up' or 'down'.

- ball_direction: The direction in which the actual golf ball moves. Another string variable, it can be either 'left' or 'right'.

- flag_distance: The flag position, a random number between 18 and 30.

- flag_x: The flag's x coordinate.

143

- `Hole`: The number of the hole currently being played.

- `hole_strokes`: A list to store the score for each of the three holes in the round.

- `round_strokes`: Total number of strokes taken for the current round.

- `in_the_hole`: A Boolean value to represent whether or not the ball is in the hole.

Variable naming conventions

We have talked a lot about variables when designing the games in this book, but how do we decide on a variable name?

The first rule of thumb is that a variable name should clearly indicate the purpose of the variable. Looking at golf, we have variables called `in_the_hole`, `flag_distance`, `round_strokes`, and so on. These are meaningful variable names. When computers were much less powerful than they are today, variable names were kept as short as possible, and it would be common for a program to be littered with variable names like `a`, `i`, and `x`. This made the code much harder to read.

Second, to further aid readability in Python programs, we use what is known as snake case. Using snake case, we write our variable names in lower case with underscores instead of spaces.

Constants

But what about these variables that are capitalized? These are known as constants. Unlike normal variables, the value of a constant is not meant to change when the program is run. In some programming languages, it's simply not possible to change the value of a constant once it has been declared. In Python, technically the value of a constant can be changed, but we really don't want to do that. We use capital letters to make it clear that a constant is being used, and its value should not be changed by the program code.

Key learning   Variable names should be meaningful and written using snake_case.

Constant names should be capitalized, and their value should not be changed by the program code.

Step 3: Display background

As with all of the previous games, we set up a while True loop and check the Pygame events queue to see if a quit event has occurred. Then, we blit our game background at position (0,0). Add code listing 4 (Figure 13-5) to your program.

```
102    # Main game loop
103    while True:
104
105        for event in pygame.event.get():
106
107            if event.type == QUIT:
108                pygame.quit()
109                sys.exit()
110
111        # Draw background
112        game_screen.blit(background_image, [0, 0])
113
114        pygame.display.update()
115        clock.tick(30)
116
117
118    if __name__ == '__main__':
119        main()
```

Figure 13-5. *Golf code listing 4*

Step 4: Display flag

We already know that the flag will be displayed at a random distance from the tee (see line 91):

```
flag_distance = random.randint(RANDOM_FLAG_MIN, RANDOM_FLAG_MAX)
```

We also know that RANDOM_FLAG_MIN is a constant, initialized to 18, and RANDOM_FLAG_MAX is a constant initialized to 30.

So flag_distance is a random number between 18 and 30.

But what are the x and y coordinates for the flag?

To calculate the flag's x coordinate, we need to multiply the flag_distance by the number of pixels between each flag position. We already have a constant for this called FLAG_STEP which is set to 18 at line 49 of the code. Finally, to ensure that the flag is centered correctly, we need to add a few more pixels (HOLE_CENTRE) to flag_x to take into account the hole offset.

We have actually already calculated the x coordinate at line 92 of the program:

```
flag_x = flag_distance * FLAG_STEP + HOLE_CENTRE
```

The y coordinate is a bit easier because it remains the same during the game. There is a constant FLAG_Y which is set to 244 at line 46.

The only consideration now is to decide which flag to display, as there are three different flag images in the game, one for each hole.

The code in Figure 13-6 draws the correct flag at the correct position.

```
111     # Draw background
112     game_screen.blit(background_image, [0, 0])
113
114     # Draw flag
115     if hole == 1:
116         game_screen.blit(flag_1_image, [flag_x, FLAG_Y])
117     elif hole == 2:
118         game_screen.blit(flag_2_image, [flag_x, FLAG_Y])
119     elif hole == 3:
120         game_screen.blit(flag_3_image, [flag_x, FLAG_Y])
121
122     pygame.display.update()
123     clock.tick(30)
```

Figure 13-6. *Golf code listing 5*

Run the program a few times, and the flag will appear in a different location each time.

In the next chapter, we will develop the code to move the power meter and hit the ball.

## CHAPTER 14

Golf part 2: On the green

'And that's a delightful shot from Johnson there, Jim. Both players have found the green in two.'

'It sure was, Corey. Johnson is sitting about 18 feet from the hole with Miller maybe only 10 feet away, but with a trickier downhill putt. You can cut the tension here with a knife...'

In the last chapter, we completed the setup and displayed the flag in a random position. In this chapter, we will complete the following steps:

5. Power meter.

6. Move the ball.

Step 5: Power meter

The power meter is used to determine the strength of the player's shot. The easiest solution would have been to have the player type in a number between 1 and 30. However, we will use a power meter to make hitting a shot that bit more difficult, and the game will look much better too.

Let's begin by updating the slider on the power meter. The code in Figure 14-1 shows how this is done.

© Mark Cunningham 2020
M. Cunningham, *Game Programming with Code Angel,*
https://doi.org/10.1007/978-1-4842-5305-2_14

```
106             for event in pygame.event.get():
106
107                 if event.type == QUIT:
108                     pygame.quit()
109                     sys.exit()
110
111             # Update slider
112             slider_timer -= 1
113
114             if slider_timer == 0:
115
116                 # Slider moving up, increase shot power
117                 if slider_direction == 'up':
118                     shot_power += 1
119                     if shot_power == MAX_POWER:
120                         slider_direction = 'down'
121
122                 # Slider moving down, decrease shot power
123                 elif slider_direction == 'down':
124                     shot_power -= 1
125                     if shot_power == MIN_POWER:
126                         slider_direction = 'up'
127
128                 # New timer pause
129                 if shot_power <= SLOW_PUTT_RANGE:
130                     slider_timer = SLOW_SLIDER_SPEED
131                 else:
132                     slider_timer = SLIDER_SPEED
133
134             # Draw background
135             game_screen.blit(background_image, (0, 0))
```

Figure 14-1. *Golf code listing 6*

The variable `slider_timer` is a timer which handles the delay as the slider moves from one bar on the meter to the next. Line 112 subtracts one from the timer each frame. If the timer reaches 0 (line 114), we do two things:

1. Move the slider up or down.

2. Start a new timer.

Let's look at how we move the slider first of all.
Line 117 tests the `slider_direction` to see if it equals `'up'`.
If the slider is moving up

- Line 118 increases the `shot_power` by 1.

- Line 119 checks to see if the `shot_power` has reached the `MAX_POWER` (set to 30 at the start of the program). If `shot_power` equals `MAX_POWER,` then we set `slider_direction` to `'down'` so that the slider starts moving downward.

If the slider is not moving up, then line 123 tests `slider_direction` to see if it equals `'down'`.

If the slider is moving down

- Line 124 decreases the `shot_power` by 1.

- Line 125 checks to see if the `shot_power` has reached the `MIN_POWER` (set to 1 at the start of the program). If `shot_power` equals `MIN_POWER`, then we change the direction of the slider to `'up'`.

Irrespective of whether the slider is moving up or down, if `slider_timer` has reached 0, then we need a new timer. The duration of this new timer is dependent on the current value of `shot_power`. Remember, when the slider is at the bottom of the power meter, we want it to take a little longer moving from one bar to the next. Lines 129–132 show how we achieve this:

- Line 129 tests to see if `shot_power <= SLOW_PUTT_RANGE`, which is a constant used to determine when the slider should move more slowly. We can see from line 36 that `SLOW_PUTT_RANGE` is 3. Therefore, if `shot_power` equals 1, 2, or 3, then the new `slider_timer` will be set to `SLOW_SLIDER_SPEED` (which is 20).

- However, we can see that if the `shot_power` is anything above 3, the new `slider_timer` will be set to `SLIDER_SPEED` (which is 5). This means that the speed of the slider on bars 4–30 of the power meter will be four times as fast as the speed of the slider on bars 1–3.

You can change the values of `SLIDER_SPEED` and `SLOW_SLIDER_SPEED` to make the game easier or more difficult.

Of course, all of this is going on in the background. We won't see anything happen until we display the power meter and slider. The code in Figure 14-2 shows how to do this.

```
136     # Draw background
137     game_screen.blit(background_image, [0, 0])
138
137     # Draw meter and slider
138     if ball_distance == 0 and in_the_hole is False:
139         game_screen.blit(power_meter_image, [METER_X, METER_Y])
140
141         slider_step = (MAX_POWER - shot_power) * meter_height / MAX_POWER
142         slider_y = METER_Y + SLIDER_BORDER + slider_step - SLIDER_TOP_PADDDING
143         game_screen.blit(slider_image, [SLIDER_X, slider_y])
144
145     # Draw flag
146     if hole == 1:
147         game_screen.blit(flag_1_image, [flag_x, FLAG_Y])
148     elif hole == 2:
149         game_screen.blit(flag_2_image, [flag_x, FLAG_Y])
150     elif hole == 3:
151         game_screen.blit(flag_3_image, [flag_x, FLAG_Y])
```

Figure 14-2. *Golf code listing 7*

First up, we only want to display the power meter if the ball has not
been hit and the ball is not in the hole. Line 138 checks these conditions
and if they are both met:

- Line 139 displays the `power_meter`.

- Lines 141 and 142 do some basic math to work out the
  y coordinate of the slider depending on the value of
  `shot_power`.

- Line 143 `blits` the slider image onto the screen.

Run the program, and you should see the slider moving up and down
the power meter, and it will move more slowly when it reaches the bottom.

Step 6: Move the ball

The player must judge how much power their golf shot requires. If they hit
their shot while the slider is near the bottom of the power meter, the ball
will go a very short distance. Hitting a shot when the slider is near the top
of the power meter means the ball will go much further. The player hits the
ball by tapping the spacebar.

Let's write the code to handle the spacebar event as shown in
Figure 14-3.

```
102      # Main game loop
103      while True:
104
105          for event in pygame.event.get():
106              key_pressed = pygame.key.get_pressed()
107
108              # SPACE key pressed - hit shot
109              if key_pressed[pygame.K_SPACE] and ball_distance == 0 and in_the_hole is False:
110                  slider_direction = 'none'
111                  ball_distance = shot_power * moves_per_flag
112
113                  hole_strokes[hole - 1] += 1
114
115                  if ball_direction == 'right':
116                      final_ball_location += shot_power
117                  else:
118                      final_ball_location -= shot_power
119
120                  putt_sound.play()
121
122              if event.type == QUIT:
123                  pygame.quit()
124                  sys.exit()
125
126          # Update slider
127          slider_timer -= 1
```

Figure 14-3. *Golf code listing 8*

We are familiar with the code to test if a key has been pressed. We want to hit the ball if the following three conditions have happened:

- The spacebar has been tapped.

- The ball_distance is 0 (this means the ball is not already moving).

- in_the_hole is False (the ball is not already in the hole).

If all three of the conditions are true, we write some code to prepare moving the ball. This code between lines 110 and 120 can be explained as follows:

- Line 110 sets slider_direction to 'none' to stop the slider moving up or down.

- Line 111 calculates the total number of pixels that the ball will move by multiplying the shot_power (the value of the slider on the power meter) by the moves_per_flag (the number of pixels between each flag position). The result is stored in the variable ball_distance which we will use when actually moving the ball.

153

- Line 113 adds one onto the number of strokes in the hole. We will look at this line in a bit more depth shortly.

- Line 115 tests to see if the ball is moving right and then calculates the final location of the ball by adding the shot power onto the current location of the ball.

- The else statement at line 117 means that the ball_direction is not 'right', and so it must be 'left'. In this case, the final ball location is calculated by subtracting the shot power from the current ball location.

- Lastly, line 120 plays a sound effect of the ball hitting the golf club.

More about lists

We looked briefly at *lists* when we wrote Forest Bomber, but it's time to consider them in a bit more detail.

A list in Python is a container which can hold multiple elements or objects. To create a list, we write the elements between square brackets, separated by commas.

In Golf, we use the list hole_strokes to store the number of strokes taken at each hole. We initialize the hole_strokes list like this:

```
hole_strokes = [0, 0, 0]
```

So the hole_strokes list has three elements.

Each item in a list can be identified by its *index*, but it should be noted that the index always starts at 0 and not 1. So the three elements in the hole_strokes list have indexes 0, 1, and 2, respectively.

Should we wish to access a list element, we place its index in square brackets.

So to access the first element in our `hole_strokes` list, we use

`hole_strokes[0]`

To access the third and last element in our `hole_strokes` list, we use

`hole_strokes[2]`

Let's look again at the code which we used to update the number of strokes for the hole when the ball was hit. It's at line 113:

`hole_strokes[hole - 1] += 1`

Assuming we are on the first hole, the hole will equal 1. We want to add 1 to the value of the first element of our list. But remember the index always starts at 0, so actually we want to add one to `hole_strokes[0]`. Using `hole - 1` as the index means we will reference index 0 for hole 1, index 1 for hole 2, and index 2 for hole 3.

After the first shot has been hit, we add 1 onto `hole_strokes[0]`, and so the list will become

[1, 0, 0]

Key learning   A list is a variable which can hold multiple elements.

We reference individual list items by using their index.

List indexes start at 0.

Update ball location

All we have done so far is get the ball ready to move. Now we need to move it across the screen by the distance determined by the power meter. The actual distance to be moved has already been calculated and stored in the variable `ball_distance`. Enter code listing 9 (Figure 14-4).

```
# New timer pause
if shot_power <= SLOW_PUTT_RANGE:
    slider_timer = SLOW_SLIDER_SPEED
else:
    slider_timer = SLIDER_SPEED

# Update ball location
if ball_distance > 0:

    if ball_direction == 'right':
        ball_x += BALL_STEP
    else:
        ball_x -= BALL_STEP

    # Ball gone off left or right hand edge of screen
    if ball_x > SCREEN_WIDTH or ball_x < 0:

        # Reset ball location at left of screen
        ball_x = START_BALL_X
        ball_distance = 0
        ball_direction = 'right'
        shot_power = 1

        # Reset slider at bottom of meter
        slider_direction = 'up'
        final_ball_location = 0
        slider_timer = SLOW_SLIDER_SPEED

    # Ball is still on screen so move ball closer to final_ball_position
    else:
        ball_distance -= 1

        # Ball has stopped rolling
        if ball_distance == 0:

            # Ball in hole
            if final_ball_location == flag_distance:
                in_the_hole = True
                round_strokes += hole_strokes[hole - 1]

                clap_sound.play()

            # Ball missed hole
            else:
                if final_ball_location < flag_distance:
                    ball_direction = 'right'
                else:
                    ball_direction = 'left'

                # Reset slider at bottom of meter
                shot_power = 1
                slider_direction = 'up'
                slider_timer = SLOW_SLIDER_SPEED

# Draw background
game_screen.blit(background_image, [0, 0])
```

Figure 14-4. *Golf code listing 9*

As you can see, there is quite a bit of code in Figure 14-4, so let's take a closer look at what it does.

Line 150 checks to see if `ball_distance` > 0. The variable `ball_distance` is greater than zero when the ball is moving. It will become zero when it reaches its final destination and therefore stop moving.

Lines 152–155 update the ball's x coordinate (stored in `ball_x`). If the ball is moving to the right, we add to the x coordinate, and if the ball is moving to the left, we subtract from the x coordinate. The amount the ball moves each time is held in the constant BALL_STEP. BALL_STEP was initialized to 3 at the start of the program, so the ball moves 3 pixels on each frame.

There is an `if` statement at line 158 which tests the ball's x coordinate to see

- If it is greater than SCREEN_WIDTH: Which means the ball has rolled off the right-hand edge of the screen.

- If it is less than 0: Which means the ball has rolled of the left-hand edge of the screen.

The code at lines 161–169 will handle the `ball rolling off` the edge of the screen:

- Line 161 places the ball back at the tee by setting `ball_x` to START_BALL_X.

- Line 162 resets `ball_distance` to 0, because the ball should no longer be moving.

- Line 163 sets the `ball_direction` to go right.

- Line 164 resets the `shot_power` on the power meter to 1.

- Lines 167–169 reset the power meter values so that the slider starts back at the bottom.

If however the ball has not rolled off the edge of the screen, then we need to update its location each frame. The code between lines 172–195 will do this:

- Line 173 subtracts 1 from the `ball_distance`, because the ball has moved 1 place closer to the hole.

- Line 176 checks to see if `ball_distance` has become 0; in other words, the ball has reached its destination.

If the ball has reached its destination, we check to see if it has ended up in the hole. This will happen if the `final_ball_location` is equal to the `flag_distance`. If the ball is in the hole, we

- Set the Boolean `in_the_hole` to `True`.

- Add the number of strokes for the hole to the overall `round_strokes`.

- Play the sound of the crowd clapping.

If the ball is not in the hole, we

- Update the direction so that if the ball is to the left of the flag, the direction will become `'right'`, or if the ball is to the right of the flag, the direction will become `'left'`.

- Reset the slider so that it starts at the bottom of the power meter.

Draw the ball

For us to see all of this code in action, we need to actually draw the ball. Enter the code from Figure 14-5.

```
308       # Draw flag
309       if hole == 1:
310           game_screen.blit(flag_1_image, (flag_x, FLAG_Y))
311       elif hole == 2:
312           game_screen.blit(flag_2_image, (flag_x, FLAG_Y))
313       elif hole == 3:
314           game_screen.blit(flag_3_image, (flag_x, FLAG_Y))
315
316       # Draw ball
317       if in_the_hole is False:
318           game_screen.blit(ball_image, (ball_x, BALL_Y))
319       else:
320           game_screen.blit(ball_image, (ball_x, BALL_Y + BALL_DESCENT))
321
322       pygame.display.update()
323       clock.tick(30)
```

Figure 14-5. Golf code listing 10

The code in Figure 14-5 is fairly straightforward. The only aspect that
is worth further note is at line 220 where we add BALL_DESCENT to the ball's
y coordinate (BALL_Y) if the ball has landed in the hole. By moving the ball
down the screen a few pixels, it will give the effect of the ball dropping into
the hole.

Run the game and see if you can get the ball in the hole.

In the next and final chapter of the book, we will pull the remaining
parts of the game together so that our Golf game runs for all three holes.

CHAPTER 15

Golf part 3: It's in the hole

'Incredible scenes here as Tommy Miller's putt comes up short by what can only be an inch. And so now Mitch Johnson has this 18-foot putt for the Open Championship. Over to you, Jim.'

'Yes, Corey, the crowd hold their breath as Johnson stands over the ball. He sends it forward, but does it have the legs? It's going... It's going...'

'It's...'

'in...'

'the...'

'HOLE!'

We have built most of the mechanics for our Golf game. Now we just need to add the last parts of our code to finish it off. The remaining steps are

7. In the hole

8. Scoreboard

© Mark Cunningham 2020
M. Cunningham, *Game Programming with Code Angel*,
https://doi.org/10.1007/978-1-4842-5305-2_15

Step 7: In the hole

In actual fact, we have already worked out if the ball is in the hole. Look back at lines 179 and 180 where we set in_the_hole to True if the final_ball_location was equal to the flag_distance.

First of all, we need to display a message if the ball is in the hole. We will use a function to do this. Add the in_hole_message function shown in code listing 11 (Figure 15-1) to your program.

```
216          # Draw ball
217          if in_the_hole is False:
218              game_screen.blit(ball_image, [ball_x, BALL_Y])
219          else:
220              game_screen.blit(ball_image, [ball_x, BALL_Y + BALL_DESCENT])
221
222          pygame.display.update()
223          clock.tick(30)
224
225
226  # Display message at the end of each hole
227  def in_hole_message(hole_number, hole_strokes, round_strokes):
228
229      if hole_number == 3:
230          message = 'Round completed in ' + str(round_strokes) + '. Press RETURN to play another round.'
231          text = font.render(message, True, WHITE)
232      else:
233          message = 'In the hole in ' + str(hole_strokes) + '. Press RETURN to play next hole.'
234          text = font.render(message, True, WHITE)
235
236      background_x = SCOREBOARD_MARGIN * 4
237      background_width = SCREEN_WIDTH - SCOREBOARD_MARGIN * 8
238      background_height = 2 * SCOREBOARD_LINE
239      message_background_rect = [background_x, HOLE_MESSAGE_Y, background_width, background_height]
240      pygame.draw.rect(game_screen, GREY, message_background_rect)
241
242      text_rect = text.get_rect()
243      messsage_x = (SCREEN_WIDTH - text_rect.width) / 2
244      message_y = HOLE_MESSAGE_Y + SCOREBOARD_LINE / 2
245      game_screen.blit(text, [messsage_x, message_y])
246
247
248  if __name__ == '__main__':
249      main()
```

Figure 15-1. *Golf code listing 11*

Let's look more closely at this function. We can split it into three main parts:

- Lines 229–234 compose the message to be displayed depending on whether or not all three holes have been completed.

- Lines 236–240 create a rectangle to give the message a background and then blit it onto the screen.

- Lines 242–245 work out where to display the message so that it is centered horizontally.

There are some useful coding techniques used here which merit further investigation.

Joining strings

Look again at lines 230 and 233. They use the variable `message` to store the message that is to be displayed. `message` is a string, and it is composed of three parts:

- Start string: 'In the hole in'
- The number of strokes
- End string: '. Press RETURN to play the next hole.'

If the player completed the holes in four strokes, message would be assigned the following:

'In the hole in 4 strokes. Press RETURN to play the next hole.'

Did you notice how we have used the addition symbol (+) to join multiple strings together?

However, while the start string and end string are already strings, the variable `hole_strokes` is an integer. (Remember an integer stores a whole number). In Python, we cannot directly join an integer onto a string, so we first have to convert the integer to a string. You can see we convert `hole_strokes` to a string by using Python's `str()` function.

Drawing Pygame shapes

In Pygame, we can draw a range of different shapes including lines, circles, polygons, and rectangles.

To draw a rectangle, we use the `pygame.draw.rect()` function which requires three parameters:

- The surface on which to draw the rectangle, in our case `game_screen`

- The color, in our case `GREY`

- The rectangle object which holds the top-left x, top-left y, width, and height of the rectangle to be drawn

Line 239 creates the rectangle shape, while line 240 actually draws the rectangle.

Centering text

In all of our games, we have centered text on the screen, but how do we do that? There are four steps involved, as we can demonstrate by looking at lines 238, 246, and 247 of the Golf code:

1. Render the text as a surface object (line 238).

2. Get the rectangle properties of the text object using `get_rect()` (line 246).

3. Subtract the width property of the text rectangle from the overall screen width (`SCREEN_WIDTH - text_rect.width`, line 247).

4. Divide this value by 2 (line 247), and this will give the x coordinate at which the text should be displayed so that it is centered.

Drawing Pygame text

Lines 242–244 work out the x and y coordinates of the text message to be displayed so that it is centered.

Line 245 draws the message held in the variable text onto the game_ screen at the coordinates [message_x,message_y].

In the hole message

We need to write the code to call our in_hole_message function.

```
# Draw ball
if in_the_hole is False:
    game_screen.blit(ball_image, [ball_x, BALL_Y])
else:
    game_screen.blit(ball_image, [ball_x, BALL_Y + BALL_DESCENT])

# In the hole messages
if in_the_hole is True:
    in_hole_message(hole, hole_strokes[hole - 1], round_strokes)

pygame.display.update()
clock.tick(30)
```

***Figure 15-2.** Golf code listing 12*

Add the code shown in Figure 15-2 to display a message once the ball is in the hole.

So far our game only plays one hole of golf, and we want the final game to run over three holes. When the ball is in the hole, we need the user to hit return to continue. Enter the code shown in Figure 15-3.

```
108      # SPACE key pressed - hit shot
109      if key_pressed[pygame.K_SPACE] and ball_distance == 0 and in_the_hole is False:
110          slider_direction = 'none'
111          ball_distance = shot_power * moves_per_flag
112
113          hole_strokes[hole - 1] += 1
114
115          if ball_direction == 'right':
116              final_ball_location += shot_power
117          else:
118              final_ball_location -= shot_power
119
120          putt_sound.play()
121
122      # RETURN pressed when ball is in the hole - start new hole
123      elif key_pressed[pygame.K_RETURN] and in_the_hole is True:
124
125          if hole == 3:
126
127              if round_strokes < best_round_strokes or best_round_strokes == 0:
128                  best_round_strokes = round_strokes
129
130              hole = 1
131              hole_strokes = [0, 0, 0]
132              round_strokes = 0
133
134          else:
135              hole += 1
136
137          in_the_hole = False
138          shot_power = 1
139          slider_direction = 'up'
140
141          ball_x = START_BALL_X
142          ball_direction = 'right'
143          final_ball_location = 0
144
145          flag_distance = random.randint(RANDOM_FLAG_MIN, RANDOM_FLAG_MAX)
146          flag_x = flag_distance * FLAG_STEP + HOLE_CENTRE
147
148          slider_timer = SLOW_SLIDER_SPEED
149
150      if event.type == QUIT:
151          pygame.quit()
152          sys.exit()
```

Figure 15-3. *Golf code listing 13*

For this code to run, there are two conditions which have to be met in the elif statement at line 123:

- The return key must have been pressed.

- in_the_hole must be True.

If both of these conditions have occurred, then we check to see if the game has played three holes at line 125. If all three holes have been played

- We set a new best score (best_round_strokes) at lines 127 and 128. This is similar to setting a new high score in the way we have done in our previous games, but of course in golf a low score is the best score.

- We then reset the main game variables hole, hole_strokes, and round_strokes at lines 130–132 so that we can start a new game.

If all three holes have not yet been played, we will run the else statement at line 134 and add one onto the current hole number at line 135.

Finally, whether we are starting a new game or just a new hole, we set the variables for a new hole and ensure that the power meter starts at position 1 (lines 137–148). Most importantly here, we initialize a new random flag position at lines 145 and 146.

Step 8: Scoreboard

The final aspect of our game is to display a scoreboard. On the scoreboard, we want to show

- The strokes taken for each of the three holes

- The running total of the strokes for this round

- The best score for any round

We will use two functions to achieve this, display_scoreboard and display_scoreboard_data. These functions should be inserted after the main program, but before the in_hole_message function. Remember to use double line spacing between each function. Code listing 15 (Figure 15-4) and code listing 16 (Figure 15-5) should be added to your program.

```
258     # Display the scoreboard
259     def display_scoreboard(hole_strokes, round_strokes, best):
260
261         scoreboard_background_rect = (0, 0, SCREEN_WIDTH, SCOREBOARD_HEIGHT)
262         pygame.draw.rect(game_screen, GREY, scoreboard_background_rect)
263
264         # Display holes 1-3
265         display_scoreboard_data('Hole:', 0, 0)
266
267         for hole_number in range(1, 4):
268             display_scoreboard_data(str(hole_number), hole_number, 0)
269
270         # Display strokes on each of the 3 holes
271         display_scoreboard_data('Strokes:', 0, 1)
272
273         for hole_number in range(0, 3):
274             if hole_strokes[hole_number] > 0:
275                 display_scoreboard_data(str(hole_strokes[hole_number]), hole_number + 1, 1)
276             else:
277                 display_scoreboard_data(str('-'), hole_number + 1, 1)
278
279         # Display total for round
280         display_scoreboard_data('Total', 6, 0)
281
282         if round_strokes > 0:
283             display_scoreboard_data(str(round_strokes), 6, 1)
284         else:
285             display_scoreboard_data(str('-'), 6, 1)
286
287         # Display best overall round
288         display_scoreboard_data('Best', 7, 0)
289
290         if best > 0:
291             display_scoreboard_data(str(best), 7, 1)
292         else:
293             display_scoreboard_data(str('-'), 7, 1)
```

Figure 15-4. *Golf code listing 15*

```
296     # Display scoreboard text items
297     def display_scoreboard_data(scoreboard_text, column, line):
298
299         display_text = font.render(scoreboard_text, True, WHITE)
300
301         text_x = SCREEN_WIDTH / SCOREBOARD_COLUMNS * column + SCOREBOARD_MARGIN
302         text_y = SCOREBOARD_MARGIN + line * SCOREBOARD_LINE
303
304         game_screen.blit(display_text, (text_x, text_y))
```

Figure 15-5. *Golf code listing 16*

The scoreboard is split into ten equal columns as defined by
SCOREBOARD_COLUMNS.

The function `display_scoreboard_data` takes three parameters:

- The text to be displayed

- The column number at which the text should be displayed

- The line on which to display the text (0 or 1)

The function carries out some basic arithmetic on these parameters to work out the co-ordinates of each scoreboard element.

We can then call the function with code, for example, line 280:

```
display_scoreboard_data('Total', 6, 0)
```

This will display the text 'Total' at column 6 on line 0 of the scoreboard.

Fixed loops

In programming, a fixed loop will repeat a block of code a specific number of times. In Python, we use the `for` keyword when writing a fixed loop.

Let's take a closer look at the code at line 267:

```
for hole_number in range (1, 4):
```

This code uses a `for` loop to repeat a fixed number of times, in this case three. Each time through the loop, the variable `hole_number` will be increased by 1. In other words, `hole_number` will be

- 1 the first time through the loop

- 2 the second time through the loop

- 3 the third time through the loop

Note that the loop will run three times (and not four times). A Python for loop will repeat up to (but not including) the stop value, which in this example is 4. So our loop starts at 1 and goes up to (but not including) 4.

It is possible to use different start and stop values for a fixed loop, for example

- `for number in range (10, 20)` will loop ten times. number will start at 10 and increase each time through the loop, ending on 19.

- `for number in range (0, 10, 2)` will loop five times and go up in increments of 2. As the loop repeats, number will have the values 0, 2, 4, 6, and 8.

Key learning   A fixed loop repeats a given number of times.

In Python, fixed loops use the for keyword.

Use range to give the loop a start and stop value.

Display the scoreboard

We need to add some code to call the `display_scoreboard` function and display the scoreboard.

```
244        # Draw ball
245        if in_the_hole is False:
246            game_screen.blit(ball_image, (ball_x, BALL_Y))
247        else:
248            game_screen.blit(ball_image, (ball_x, BALL_Y + BALL_DESCENT))
249
250        # Display scoreboard
251        display_scoreboard(hole_strokes, round_strokes, best_round_strokes)
252
253        # In the hole messages
254        if in_the_hole is True:
255            in_hole_message(hole, hole_strokes[hole - 1], round_strokes)
```

Figure 15-6. *Golf code listing 17*

Add the code shown in Figure 15-6 and run the program. Grab your clubs and go and play a round of golf.

Wrapping up

Congratulations! If you have reached this far in the book, you have programmed four computer games in Python/Pygame.

Don't worry if you found some parts of the code hard to understand; that is only to be expected. Computer programming is not easy, and it takes time and practice to become a good coder.

Try to take some of the skills you have learned from this book and create your own game. Don't try and do everything at once though, but build your game up in steps, as we have done throughout this book. Building games and programs in this way allows you to test each stage before moving on to the next.

Good luck...

Index

A

Alien invasion, 2
    game environment setup
        code, 103
        constants, 104, 105
        display background, 108
        initialize variables, 106, 107
    screen design, 103
    steps, 102
    UFOs, 101

B

Bugs, 3, 5

C

check_ufo_hit function, 130
Comparison operators, 111

D, E

Debugging, 5
def main(), 65
display_game_over
    function, 98, 135
display_scoreboard_data
    function, 98, 169

Display scoreboard, Forest Bomber
    background
        code, 50
        game_screen, 51
        information, 51
        rectangle, 50
        values, 51
    high score, 54, 55
    level, 53, 54
    messages
        circumstances, 56
        code, 57, 58
        else statement, 57
        level_cleared, 56
        plane_exploded, 56
        Pygame, 57
        tests, 56
    score, 52–53
display_scoreboard function, 170
Drop bomb, Forest Bomber
    Boolean variables, 43
    else if, 44
    exploding trees, 40–42
    ground level, 42, 43
    if statement, 46
    key presses
        code, 34
        if statement, 35

© Mark Cunningham 2020
M. Cunningham, *Game Programming with Code Angel*,
https://doi.org/10.1007/978-1-4842-5305-2

P, Q

Printed in the United States
By Bookmasters